Good Grief Revised, Updated and Expanded

Ending Up in the Divine Embrace

By Dr. Nancy Moelk

©Firehouse Ministries, Inc. 2020
Revised© 2019 Firehouse Ministries, Inc.
Revised© 2017 Firehouse Ministries, Inc.
Originally Published as Good Grief by Firehouse Ministries, Inc. 2003

ISBN⁻978-0-9984660-8-8
Published by Firehouse Ministries, Inc.
Printed in the United States of America
Other resources are available at firehouseminstries.com
Email: firehousemoelk@comcast.net

©Firehouse Ministries, Inc. 2020
Cover Art by Dr. Nancy Moelk, 12/12/19, "You are Never Alone".

To all those who have helped me grieve
in my soul's journey so to
continually end up in the Divine Embrace

Notably

Gary Moelk, husband,
Richard Kinney, co-worker and friend,
Dr. Mario Rivera Mendez, pastor and counselor

Contents

Forward

This manuscript was originally written in 1994. My understanding and development have grown since that time and I wanted to expand the original content in the hopes of creating a more effective tool to draw people into God's embrace. I have added several new chapters which give further help to cleanse the soul from toxins that pollute our lives and relationships. My co-worker, Richard Kinney, provided the insights for much of the chapters on resignation and the spirit man. These additions greatly enrich and help anyone seeking to move through their losses back to joy.

I first learned about how our past remains active in our current lives from several people's work: Dr. Mario Rivera, Alice Miller, Dr. Daniel Goldman, and various periodical articles referring to the computer brain studies conducted on Romanian infants in the 1990's. Over the years, I developed these ideas by supporting it with Scripture and using it to help decipher the twisting of the human soul in its attempts to undo loss without God's help.

For years people have come to me with their unresolved grief issues. They come not knowing why they seem stuck in life, but rarely do they leave without recognizing that God has the solution for them. They admit their losses and allow His love to guide them through to resolution of those losses. The result of that is new energy and zeal for life and many hopeful possibilities without the burden of unresolved issues blocking progress.

The concept of God grieving is an original insight concerning the Person of God and how it is expressed in humans, the creation made in His image. The stages of grief are based on the Kubler-Ross model as expressed in her 1969 book *On Death and Dying*. Although not every culture grieves exactly alike, all people on the planet go through a similar version of a grief process for significant life losses.

An article from the American Anthropological Association magazine, Ethos, documents the consistency of the experience of grief as well as the ability of our cultural expectations to modify the process:

The cross-cultural study of mourning offers promising ground for exploring the relationship between culture and emotional experience. Researchers have documented the profound feelings of grief, anger, and fear that accompany losses everywhere, suggesting that there is a "core grieving process" that occurs across cultures.[1]

As Christians, our grieving is really a transformational process by which we can have a life full of joy, pleasure and success. If we have been separated from all the benefits of God's active presence in our lives by our unresolved issues, this book can provide encouragement and direction for getting us into that wonderful Divine Embrace.

---

[1]Brison, K. J. and Leavitt, S. C. (1995), Coping with Bereavement: Long-Term Perspectives on Grief and Mourning. Ethos, 23. p. 395

*For every thousand hacking at the leaves of
evil, there is one striking at the root.*[2]

Henry David Thoreau

---

[2] Common Paraphrase from HENRY DAVID THOREAU, Walden, chapter 1, p. 98 (1966). Originally published in 1854.

Intro: Why Read This Book?

How can grief be "good"? What is positive about grieving? Grieving is a way to come alive to yourself, to God, to your life. It's important to remember that grief is a passage to joy and a deeper life—not your new home. No one wants you to camp out in grief, but that is exactly what you will end up doing if you don't allow the natural grieving process God has placed within to set you free.

The body knows how to heal itself from a cut or a broken bone. You may be sore, bruised and tired as you mend, but if given a chance, the body will usually heal itself. The emotions similarly have a mechanism to heal themselves. That is the process of grief. We cannot avoid some sorrow and grief in this life, but we can learn to be healed from life losses and learn to move forward stronger and more beautiful.

The Bible repeatedly speaks of a pattern of good results from sorrow and grief:

Jesus, the author and finisher of our faith, who for the joy that was set before Him endured the cross[3]

A woman has pain in childbirth because her time has come; but when she brings forth her child, she forgets her anguish because of her joy that a child has been born into the world.[4]

Blessed are those who mourn, for they shall be comforted.[5]

---

[3] Hebrews 12:2, NKJV
[4] John 16:21, Berean Study Bible
[5] Matthew 5:4, NKJV.

Grief leads people through a valley of sorrow that creates an entrance to a place of joy and rest from the many unresolved losses in their lives. You can trade the sorrows of life for joy if only you have the right set of tools.

Good Grief Revised, Updated and Expanded contains such a set of tools.
- You will learn to grieve life losses as an avenue to joy. This will result in a deeper, more positive awareness of God, self, and others.
- You will be able to identify the repeating life patterns based on losses from the past. This will lead you to their resolution and dismissal.
- You will find the end of the grieving process brings you to God's "Divine Embrace" in the Person of Jesus Christ—a practicing of His Presence.
- You will experience that grieving is a path to internal transformation which results in an ability to engage in personal relationships that are healthy and characterized by love.

There are two parts to *Good Grief Revised, Updated and Expanded*. Part 1, *Grief*, gives a detailed description of the grieving process. For those who have never allowed themselves to face life losses and grieve them, it offers a permission and encouragement to do so. Part 1 also describes the prerequisites for the natural response of grief to flow. You will become familiar with the steps of grief and recognize them as you move forward in the grieving process. Part 1 also explains the problem of a delayed grief reaction.

You will come to see grieving as an acceptable response to loss. God grieved His losses. You will learn how He moved through the grief process as recorded in Scripture. The cross was the end of God's "good grief". As you pick up your cross in the grief process you will finally say about each loss, "It is finished." You no longer must avoid them or express them in a harmful way which can hurt others or yourself. You will be ready to move on into a happier version of you.

Part 2, *Identify and Resolve Your Past*, explains the patterns we repeat in life which keep replaying our unresolved losses. Once we recognize those repeating patterns and identify them as losses, we can finally move on. Sharing the stories of individuals6 who have broken these cycles helps to teach us the language of the heart. They demonstrate how our hearts try to settle past losses by projecting them on to our present-day relationships. Asking people in our present life to pay for the debts from our past is not in our best interest. Instead, allowing Jesus Christ to intervene and restore us where life and love have failed us gives us freedom to approach our present-day relationships with a clean slate and something to offer from what we have received.

Our goals in *Good Grief Revised, Updated and Expanded* are these:

1. To seek to access the innate grieving process within us.
2. To identify and remove barriers that block us from grieving.
3.   To allow the expression of grief that can free us to move on in life and our relationships.

Addressing these issues can be painful and difficult. But the result enables us to live a life of love.7 Removing the barriers to an experiential encounter with God's love, as characterized by his comfort and restoration, enables us to love ourselves and others. When you are no longer carrying around heavy weights of unresolved life losses, connection to the "pleasant present moment" of life becomes your "new normal". It frees you to use your energy to live fully engaged in the here and now. It also frees you to be authentic since you have no need to be constantly managing hidden burdens of pain.

This is a script for emotional health and transformation that is rooted in the Word of God: both in the written word and in the Person of Jesus Christ. Jesus said, "In the world you will have tribulation, but be of good cheer, I have overcome the world." He did that by embracing the serious losses of His creation. He picked up the pain of all those losses in the cross which led

---

[6] They are actually composites of different people I have helped over the years in my experience as a Christian prayer minister.

[7] See Ephesians 5:2. All Biblical quotations are from the New International Version unless otherwise noted.

to His dying to them. He calls us to pick up our cross of grief so we, too, can die to our life losses. The result is to become a partaker of resurrection life power in areas of our souls where loss has been undone by the power of His Presence; where forgiveness has been accomplished and where restoration of our faith, hope and love has occurred. The results are a life with joy, purpose and deep connection with His supernatural power flowing through us in ever increasing measure.

Part 1—Grief

Chapter 1—Coming Alive Through Grief

To start, I would like to help you redefine in your mind a couple of phrases you may assume you understand. The first is "the grieving process" and the second is "dying to self".

We will be discussing at length in this book the grieving process and outlining both what it is and what it is not as well as the repercussions for those who refuse to grieve. But what I want to emphasis more than anything else in this book is that real grief leads to a coming alive which far outweighs any discomfort caused by it. If you have ever been pregnant, you get this concept of how the pleasure and satisfaction of the baby in your arms helps you to quickly forget the pain endured to finally embrace him or her.

"Dying to self" is another catch phrase that people throw around, but few understand what it means. Like the process of grief, dying to self is a gateway to being fully alive and happy. It is a developmental tool, not a hateful rejection of your basic self that amputates important parts of your personality. You are a beautiful being for whom Christ was willing to die.

When Jesus spoke of His own death, He described it as "the time has come for the glory of God to surround the Son."[8] He didn't act as if the suffering was the point or an end in itself. He was focused on the wonderous reality awaiting Him afterwards, His coming alive in a whole new way—not the discomfort of the process. People who are great artists or athletes don't get far unless they focus on the joy and fulfillment of doing their gifting and the resulting rewards of that.

---

[8] John 13. Passion Translation

For instance, when you show up each day to engage God's presence[9], it isn't a horrible death to some other activity which you heroically forfeited (like extra sleep or reading the news). It is a great time of coming alive to God. You may have sacrificed to put aside the time to spend with Him But communing with Him has such rewards that it is well worth any effort. Doing exercise helps us to come alive to our bodies although, at first, it may be painful.

Discipline is the key to freedom, and the way to happy and vigorous living is submitting yourself not only to God but to the spirit man which leads to joyful union in you so that you can have joy and pleasure and a successful life. I look on that as coming alive from a state of deadness. We are not a moldering heap of death. **So, once again, grieving, a type of dying to self, is a transformational process.**

I would like to propose that when I say you need to grieve; you understand that this is a type of coming alive even though it is also a way of dying to destructive beliefs and behaviors. And in order to come alive to God we must engage in a transformational process. This is much more inviting than the word grieving or dying to self.

Jesus was a man of sorrows and acquainted with grief while He was on earth. But He focused on the amazing joy which awaited Him once the hard part was over! In our next chapter, we will examine His experience of the grief process in Scripture.

---

[9] Some call it a Quiet Time or Prayer Time.

Chapter 2—Our God Grieves

The grieving process removes barriers to an alive and vibrant life. Jesus, who had no sin, was still a man and had a soul. He submitted Himself to human form and to the losses which befall us. He cycled through the grieving process. Here is a list of illustrations of how Jesus grieved:

- Jesus was shocked and dismayed at the unbelief of the Jews.
- He was angry at their legalistic pride and greedy dealings.
- He was saddened by their history of rejecting God.
- He felt depression over the death and loss all around Him.
- He bargained by asking God if there was any way to avoid this way of resolving the loss of all the ages, but ultimately surrendered His will to the Father's.
- And then in a moment of great pain resulting from the consequences of sin and loss, He chose to forgive. He understood that these clueless people had no idea how their evil was offending God and His creation.

God demonstrates His own amazing ability to grieve in both the Old and New Testaments:

"Then the Lord saw that the wickedness of man was great in the earth, and that every intent of the thoughts of his heart was only evil continually. And the Lord was sorry that He had made man on the earth, and He was grieved in His heart."[10]

"And when He [Jesus] had looked around at them with anger, being grieved by the hardness of their hearts, He said to the man 'Stretch out your hand.'"[11]

---

[10] Genesis 6:5-6. NKJ.
[11] Mark 3:5. NKJ.

God recognized man's rebellion against Him as a loss. This is beyond our ability to fully grasp. God who is complete in Himself and without needs suffered loss at our hands. Through the prophets He proclaims His shock at the betrayal of His people.[12] His anger is expressed by sending his people into exile or allowing their enemies to triumph over them. His sadness shows itself in Him comparing His people to an unfaithful wife such as in the book of Hosea. He even bargains with His people, "Come let us reason together." His final stage of grief comes after a full sounding out of all that it has cost Him (as recorded in Scripture). At the cross God finishes His grief by forgiving the world. And forgiveness, of course, is the final stage of grief. We will discuss later Jesus moving through the process of grief. Here we are setting the pattern of how, created in God's image, we are meant to grieve. Don't forget that our mourning is meant to end in gladness.

We will follow this pattern in our lives, both for the losses we have suffered and for those we have created for others.

Just as there are many examples in the Scripture of people grieving, there are equally illustrations of those who refused to grieve.[13] King Saul demonstrates his hardness of heart to facing loss. When confronted with his sin by Samuel[14], he did three things other than grieve the losses resulting from his choices:

1. He pretended (denied) there was nothing wrong (vs. 13, 20).
2. He tried to shift the blame to others (vs. 15, 21).
3. He showed that his greatest concern was how he would appear before the people, not how his heart looked before God (vs. 25, 30).

The result of his denial separated him from God and led to God removing the kingship from his family line.

Does the crime fit the punishment; we may wonder? Saul's refusal to face what was in his heart and allow God's intervention appeared to be more

---

[12] See the prophets such as Isaiah, Jeremiah, Ezekiel, etc.
[13] In Chapter 9 we will further develop the results of impaired grief.
[14] 1 Samuel 3.

serious and redeemable than David's adultery and murder. The difference between them was that David was willing to be admit and deal with his heart before God and before the people.

When confronted with his sin, David openly confessed before the people[15] and wrote Psalm 51 to the Lord. He was familiar with the losses of his life and grieved them deeply. He was acquainted with both the effects of evil upon him as well as the evil he had inflicted on others.

It is true that David passed on significant dysfunction to his children, but he left a legacy of how to resolve conflicts by facing those losses in truth and sounding out the depths of his grief, then knowing God in that place.

May God give us the desire for "truth in the inner parts"[16]. God, give us humility to openly confess our rage, our disappointments, our fears, and our wounding in Your presence at the risk of exposing our own failures. Put us in a safe group of people who will not condemn our response to loss, but who will buffer our path through grief until our souls are restored and we live in Your presence in every area of our lives. Lead us in service that is ordained and sustained by Your resurrection power and not by our twisted drive to perform. Bear much fruit in our lives that feeds everyone who is in relationship with us.

I am convinced that God has put a blueprint in each one of us, a huge reservoir of potential that is just waiting to be discovered and developed. Grieving our losses helps to unbury the real person in there and to free them to be all they were meant to be!

---

[15] See 2 Samuel 12.
[16] Psalm 51:6a

9

Chapter 3—To Grieve or Not to Grieve

As a counselor I have run into many clients who have deep grief but nowhere to go with it. Instead of being fully alive to all that God and their life may have to offer, they walk about in a type of limbo. Many people are told to shut up or to cover their losses and grief in some artificial way. One of the worst is when you believe that because you "trust God" you shouldn't be sad, upset, hurting, etc.

Whatever your losses may be, my hope is that that this book can be a help to you in facing losses which come into every life and with this understanding you can help yourself or a loved one make the passage through grief into coming fully alive.

Grief is the pathway for recovery from any loss. Some cultures know better than others how to help each member confront their losses and grief in a way that allows the mourner to go on successfully with the rest of life. Besides grieving death, older cultures provide outlets for other losses as well.

In some, young men are ritualistically dragged from beside their wailing mothers into the initiation of life as men. At the traditional Italian wedding, there is the "last dance" for the bride with her father and for the groom with his mother. I have seen many tears at these events during those dances. These powerful and important rituals give us permission to recognize and grieve loss.

In our culture of disintegrating home and family life, there is less and less structure for any such rituals. Without them or something to take their place, there is little opportunity to grieve the changes and losses of life. If you neglect to allow the process of grief to run its course, you will have to use a certain amount of energy and focus on managing unresolved losses. This detracts from what you have available for present day effectiveness.

Both the Old and New Testaments give examples of people grieving. Sitting in sackcloth and ashes was a way to express deep grieving[17]. Joseph grieved over the rupture in his relationship with his brothers as well as their rejection.[18] Hannah grieved over her bareness.[19] Samuel grieved over the removal of God's blessing from King Saul.[20] At the tomb of Lazarus, Jesus wept, not because of his death but because of the loss of those mourning[21]. He also grieved over Jerusalem.[22] James exhorted the people of God to grieve over their sin.[23]

We may minimize the effects of loss on our lives. Or we may mistake endless talking about losses as being real grief. Our culture leans toward medicating pain and celebrating victimization—neither of these allows people to move through the stages of grief. Instead, they stay stuck.

There may be a problem for us in understanding the grieving process the way the New Testament church or the people of the Old Testament understood it. The grieving process was a regular part of their lives. Being "emotional" was considered normal when one encountered life losses. If there was a drought or if a marriage failed, the expected response was to be sad and to express grief. For biblical people this was a no-brainer. It was not necessary to explain grief to them: it was already an acceptable, "normal" way of handling loss that was allowed in their culture. And the whole point of grief was to find a way out of sorrow and to move on to fully live again.

Some glorify stoicism in our culture. People greatly admired Jackie Kennedy for not openly grieving the death of her husband. Is it noble and dignified to hide our grief? Sometimes it is necessary. Macho guy movies portray characters that typically push aside sadness or vulnerability after a

---

[17] See the book of Job.
[18] Genesis 45.
[19] I Samuel 1.
[20] I Samuel 16:1
[21] John 11.
[22] Luke 19: 41-44.
[23] James 4:9.

loss. Recently, though, some of the special ops type TV shows have begun to address the Post Traumatic Syndrome of such people and create an awareness of the need to grieve.

The choice to just be "in pain" seems crazy to most people. We choose other options:

- We medicate.
- We stay busy.
- We shove it down.
- We try to forget.
- We blame every strong reaction as being about present day life and refuse to look at any deeper roots.
- Or we shift to the other extreme of making our lives all about losses and victimization with no movement toward resolution.

Unfortunately, emotions associated with our losses can't be forgotten. It may be possible to forbid ourselves from expressing feelings related to our losses, but they return to haunt us as new relational dramas, headaches, anxiety, fatigue, depression, illness, and unwarranted outbursts of irrational anger or anxiety. We trade tears for a deceiving web of symptoms. It is easy to see how this extra unaddressed emotional baggage creates difficulty for anyone to be fully, successfully alive!

One of the main tasks of Satan and his army of demons is to keep people from being healed from their losses. He is delighted by all the ways people distract themselves from root issues and what their hearts need for real happiness and fulfillment. The father of lies is an expert in encouraging denial. This especially makes sense when you consider that the end of the grieving process results in resolution of losses and forgiveness—and ending up in deeper connection with God.

Dealing with unresolved losses opens our hearts to healthier, more effective ways of doing whatever else we do. Some Christians fear that allowing people to focus on losses will block other "missions" of the church such as evangelism, discipleship and social causes. To the contrary, effective grieving promotes authenticity and living from a heart level connection with God which brings more power and love to whatever else we are doing. It removes roadblocks to health in the soul.

Is there ever a time and place for choosing to reject sadness, depression and grief? Yes. Sometimes our negative thinking and complaining creates depression. Studies have proven that thanksgiving and appreciation create an environment in our brains that moves us toward joy. God knows what He is talking about when He instructs us to "give thanks in all things."[24] At the same time, He also told us "Blessed are those who mourn, for they shall be comforted."[25] Authenticity about what is in our hearts, when combined with dependence on and intimacy with God has a wonderful outcome!

Obviously, there is a time for every season. God will guide us to the appropriate prescriptions for each need if we can resist relying on static formulas. "One size fit all" doesn't reflect His way of doing things as displayed in the Bible.

I have often seen two opposite reactions to grief played out in people's lives. Some run from it. We have multi-billion-dollar industries that aid people in avoiding pain. All kinds of medications may replace tears or a bad mood. If anesthetics don't take the edge off, elaborate avenues of escapism can. Anything from movies ...comfort food...shopping...to pornography and sexual deviation can be diversions from inner pain.

At another extreme, people may wallow in what they think is grief. Here are those who make being victimized a lifelong distraction. Instead of taking responsibility for their loss by grieving it and moving into vibrant life, they become a crusader for the cause against whatever has created their loss. Let me go on record that I am not against movements condemning bullying, racism, and sexual harassment, to name a few. But to stay stuck in what hurt you as the defining characteristic of your life is to neglect the opportunity to move forward and embrace this day, this reality, this possibility!

---

[24] I Thessalonians 5:13, KJV.
[25] Matthew 5:2, KJV.

13

As believers we need to ask ourselves if we can allow ourselves and others a safe place to grieve. Wisdom and strength are needed to welcome and manage the process of grief. There are pat answers you hear over and over:

- Your loved one is better off in heaven now.
- Trust God.
- Be a good witness to others.
- You need to move on.

If a priority is "image," you will present a happy face. This can fool others and even perhaps ourselves. But our growth depends on having connection with the true person deep inside.

Many years ago, I counseled several pastors. One thing I liked to ask them is how many sermons they have ever given or heard on the effects of evil in our lives due to the sin of those around us. Not one could remember such a sermon. Then I asked how many sermons they've heard on our own sin and its effects. You can be sure this is a favorite topic.

Why so little on the suffering that evil produces in our lives through parents, grandparents, siblings, and friends, or society at large? Secondary to the forgiveness of sins, Jesus wanted us to be victorious when the evil of a fallen world falls upon us.

"The Father of compassion and the God of all comfort, who comforts us in all our troubles[26]," came here to know what it feels like to suffer at the hands of evil men. Does He shy away from our suffering due to evil? Are we to avoid discussing it?

In our performance-oriented minds, suffering must have a "good point." Do we believe suffering for life's traumas, such as being unwanted or ignored by parents, laughed at by school mates, passed over for a job, or being discriminated against--to name a few of the evils we may suffer--are

---

[26] 1 Corinthians 1:3b, 4a.

allowed without being judged as "soft"? Like Pharisees who split hairs over nuances, we carefully arbitrate and pass judgment on which circumstances warrant a response of pain and for which we must stoically hide any reaction. Out of touch with our true hearts, we aim for looking appropriate and maintaining image. We polish our masks and leave the heart in solitary confinement.

As Christians we can use some good and holy methods of distracting ourselves from grief. Some people force themselves to concentrate on Scripture, others seek ecstatic supernatural experiences to run from pain. Both activities can be extremely helpful at points in bringing healing. But if used to neglect our hearts while we attend to what we believe we should be, these activities can be counterproductive. It reminds me of the verse where Jesus rebukes those who have been doing all kinds of holy things like prophesizing and doing miracles in His name.[27] But He laments that He didn't know them, *He didn't know their hearts.*

Others continually go after "emotional triggers" and "deep catharsis" in the belief that reliving your pain and going over it again and again brings resolution. I have been in a type of therapy where people enjoy the drama of re-visiting their loss. Ironically, this can be another diversion from finishing the grieving process and moving on!

Our dilemma stems from a theology filtered by culture. Although we have an assurance that victory comes from Christ's suffering at Calvary, we're disarmed by our own weakness, and feel ashamed of our own pain. Though we might know enough to desire to be broken before God, we stiffen at the first twinge of breaking. Some of this may be because we have no vision for the intense life and fullness that awaits the person who has come alive through grief.

Sometimes we're ashamed of brokenness. If we feel loss, we quickly conclude that something must be wrong with us. With our concept of "the

---

[27] See Matthew 7:21-23.

abundant life" slightly misconstrued, we actually miss out on a good deal of abundance by acting like we have it when we don't.

Picking up the cross: what does that mean? If we begin to see the cross as God's culminating act of grief which ushers in great power and positivity, it suggests picking up our cross will involve recognizing and letting go of the losses in our lives for encouraging and compelling reasons.

Whether our losses are self-inflicted by bad choices or caused by the evil choices of others, they both need resolution and won't go away by themselves. Without proper handling, our losses fill us with many unsavory beliefs, emotions and toxicity which leave less room for the good stuff God has promised to us as His beloved children.

Is it possible to resolve emotional, physical and sexual abuse issues merely by addressing them with a prayer, or our reasoning, or by avoiding them? Is it human to gloss over a life of rejection and isolation, pretending that such evils have no effect on how we view God and others?

On the other hand, is it helpful to live in a toxic environment of constant feeding on the ways we have been victimized or wounded without the vision of finally putting it all to rest and moving forward in new life?

You can exist –numb, feigning joy and wearing a façade of strength, but oblivious to the conflicts buried within your soul. Or you can parade your hurts like a badge of honor with no intention of letting them go. The place where these choices hurt is in your closest relationships: spouse, children, church, and work. Do you have fragile and shallow relationships where love is not sincere or strong? That's what I had in my life for many years before I learned how to allow myself to grieve. The next chapter tells that story.

Chapter 4—My Grief Story

My introduction to grief came in a way both unexpected and jarring when I was 17 years old.

Our phone rang around 2 am. I could hear my mother moving through the hall. What was that she was saying over and over again? Something about the bed? I was still waking up and couldn't make it out. I opened my door and there she stood, looking around in disbelief.

"He's dead. He's dead. I know he's dead." I couldn't speak. "Chris. If he were alive, they wouldn't keep him there. He would go downtown."

My 24-year-old brother had been in a car accident. We headed for the local hospital where my mom worked daily as a nurse in the emergency room. She knew the routine. Seriously injured patients were immediately sent to downtown Scranton. When the hospital called and said, "Come, it's bad," she already knew what that meant.

Within a week I was back in school. My mother never spoke much about my brother's death after that and life moved on. It wasn't until many years later that I even began to unpack the grief of my brother's death, much less all the other losses I had suffered in our highly dysfunctional family. These "other" losses in life may not seem to require a grieving process but neglecting them is very problematic.

Until my thirties, I never contemplated what the "losses" in my life might be. I was a bit of a stoic. I raced through my days without a thought of such things. Events and circumstances, which should have been counted as losses, were stiffly pushed aside. As a Christian, and particularly as a missionary[28], I did not believe I was supposed to be upset (for very long anyway) by anything. Here are a few of the losses I ignored (or tried to):

---

[28] We lived in France and North Africa between 1979-1986.

- We had virtually all our possessions stolen in our initial move overseas.
- Later, in multiple moves, we lost most of our things two more times.
- My mother rejected me for deciding to be a missionary and told me she would no longer be a Christian.
- We lived under police surveillance.
- Believer friends were imprisoned and persecuted.
- One man we thought we led to Christ turned on us and tried to hurt us. Gary was pulled into the police station for interrogation.
- Other missionaries rejected us and tried to use us.

Such hardships I accepted as the cross I had to bear, period. I believed that to express my hurt and dismay over such things was to betray God and His provision. If at that time of my life I had been a remarkably mature believer with deep connection to the manifest presence of Christ, I may have been able to accept this gladly. Instead, it was steadily eroding my inner stability and confidence.

With my lips I said one thing, but my heart was far removed and living another reality. I had carried over family and cultural patterns about grieving, (not allowing myself to grieve), into my Christian life and imagined them to be "godly." This left me wearing a mask to appear to be something I was not. It also left my soul in isolation from the comfort and help of Christ.

Years earlier, when my brother died, I couldn't stop crying. No one would talk about it. So, I just stopped feeling anything. I quickly returned to school. I remember walking through my classes in a fog all that year. When a teacher walked up to me and expressed his sympathy for my loss, I blankly looked at him and answered, "What for?"

My husband and I had been missionaries in France, then Tunisia, and finally Morocco before my world came crashing in on me. When I became a Christian, I had believed that I was an entirely new creation. I expected to be completely and perfectly transformed into one who would fully experience the power and love of Christ—IN PRACTICE.

And like everything in our culture, it couldn't be good unless it was "instant". Forget process. All my focus was on what I was doing with little concern about who I was. The concept that God cared about who I was as a person more than what I was accomplishing in life evaded me at that point.

I was a firm believer in the fact that I was supposed to be "fully alive and joyful." I expected that I would walk in His peace, His joy, His patience now and forever…that the "old" me was dead and gone, and the "new" me would consistently grow into the image of Christ. I didn't expect that to be long, painful or difficult. "He's God", I told myself. "No sweat."

I thought that the prayers I prayed would be answered as I prayed them-- and I would not need to struggle any further–that my problems were over! Over time, God began showing me that much of whom I was prior to knowing Him was still very much alive and influencing my Spirit-filled life. I had been delivered out of Egypt but there was still a lot of Egypt left in me!

Who wants to be in the desert? It certainly doesn't sound like fun. But as we know, that is where the Egypt in us rises up to be addressed. Plus, the idea of crossing the desert is to bring you into the promised land. He brings us out in order to bring us in. I didn't understand what was happening to me at the time, but God allowed several circumstances in my life to wear me down. They exposed some of the many hidden contradictions within me and brought me to a place of surrender. It made me teachable. It led me to authenticity.

Two things affected me deeply. First, while I was preparing to leave for the mission field, my mother reacted by rejecting me and threatening to reject her faith if I carried through with my plans to move overseas. Confused and torn apart, I began my missionary life under a cloud. But I was committed to my ideals of loving the people and offering the Gospel and nothing would change that.

Secondly, once submerged in the Arab culture, I gradually became aware of a sense of unease. Something I couldn't identify started to stir in me. I knew that something was wrong, but it was a while before I could admit to myself what I was feeling. My outward life, everything I was doing, every decision I was making said, "I love these people I came to minister to." Yet almost everything about Arab men upset me. Deep in my heart a voice whispered, "I don't like these men." This conflict tormented me.

Instead of maturing in my faith the way I hoped, instead of becoming victorious, joyful, and fuller of love and peace and patience... I began sinking into depression and hopelessness. There seemed nothing I could do about it.

With all my heart, I knew that God was true. Philippians 1:6 became my life's verse— "He who began a good work in you will carry it on to completion until the day of Christ Jesus." I would say that promise to myself repeatedly. Every night, unable to sleep, I'd get up to read my Bible and for hours I would pray, meditate, memorize Scripture, and make up little songs to comfort my heart. Despite all my efforts, I continued moving further into depression.

Finally, I could hold it all together no longer. We were living in a country totally hostile to believers[29], and we were being watched by the police. Keeping up the charade didn't work in these circumstances. The cracks in the foundation of a bridge go undiscovered until enough weight passes over to highlight them. The weight of our ministry was exposing the weakness in my foundation.

Though daily I taught the Bible to others, I wasn't seeing these truths impact my life the practical way I thought they should. I was pretending to be something I wasn't. While riding the crest of this conflict, with my hope at an all-time low, we had to go home for furlough. Soon we discovered that

---

[29] In 1983 Marrakesh, a city of 3 million, had approximately 30 known Moroccan Christians. Any hint of faith in Christ or evangelism could lead to a jail sentence.

we would not return to what had once been our life's call. Our application for a visa to return to Morocco was denied. This was another major loss I couldn't face or effectively address.

I felt like a total failure. But being a failure and negative feelings around seeing myself as a failure had no place in my theology. It implied either God had failed, or I was all wrong, horribly wrong, beyond redemption. I saw no solution to my dilemma. I was stuck.

How little I understood the human soul in those days. Everything was about outside appearances and performance and productivity. In a classic missionary organization such as ours, you needed to be accomplishing something. There were no medic treatments on the battlefield. No one cared about the person underneath, or the suffering. And neither did I. But no matter how much I wanted to shove down and avoid my negative perceptions and emotions, they were determined to not forget me. My basic nature as a human being was winning the battle towards authenticity no matter how I tried to hold it back.

You see, certain things about our nature just are whether we want to face it or not. We were created by One much higher, a Master Craftsman who made us children who reflect His nature. And just as the grieving process has been part of this nature, so, too the desire to be loved, to be known, to belong, has been written on our DNA. Regardless of who we are or where we come from, whatever our personality type happens to be or even what birth defects might mark us as "different," we all have similar desires and needs. It's the basic package—the human condition, though marred, is still a divine reflection.

In a sinful world, deception influences our lives, blurring God's truths. Our world flourishes with illusions and delusions, a breeding ground for deceit and despair. Some come to believe that you really don't require love… you don't need to belong… and that grief is both avoidable and unnecessary.

Others mistake common interests or causes for intimacy and real connection. Just because you bring your negative emotions or traumatic

21

events to the light doesn't automatically dissolve their power over you. Nor does a meeting, prayer or a sermon. We can hide behind many devices: a TV, a computer, endless activities, games, drinks and buffets or religious activity and social causes. If we wear a mask long enough, we can come to believe that it really is us. That will leave us lonely and lacking the connections necessary for personal growth and transformation.

You may reason, "I'm not going to sit around and feel sorry for myself." This truly sounds good, but it, too, stems from illusions. Grieving does not include wallowing in self-pity or whining out of a victim mentality. We might assume people are grieving because we always find them in a depressed and mournful state, yet this is not the healing process of grief.

Similarly, people with chronic anger, openly raging or resorting to backhanded ways to strike out at others do not model grieving either. These people portray conditions and lifestyles caused by their resistance to grief. If you vow, "I'm never going to be like them" and choose to avoid your pain, ironically, you end up becoming like them—you just won't admit it to yourself.

You can only be where you are. Facing the truth about yourself is not sin. Denying it is. Denial says that you are above needs and feelings. You may pretend losses never really bother you because you are a "super-human". Or if you tend to continually emit emotions without resolving anything, this may be a sign you are using catharsis and focusing on the past to avoid the final stages of grief. Truth is… there's only one type of human—the one that God made in His image. And our God grieved—so we were also meant to grieve. Now I want to look at some of the types of loss and pain we need to grieve in order to move into being fully and joyfully alive.

Chapter 5—Loss and Pain

Imagine your life is like a hot air balloon that was created to soar and ride on the wind of the Holy Spirit. Now picture loss and pain being sandbags in the basket of the balloon blocking you from getting very far above the ground. The process of grief is the mechanism whereby we dump the excess weight and become capable of flying high with effective living and success.

So, what exactly is grief? The term *grief* refers to the progression of emotions produced in a person after he/she has suffered a loss. Loss is unavoidable in our world which falls far short of "the way it should be". All loss creates pain; and conversely—all pain results from loss. In other words, our pain universally and unequivocally points back to loss—real or perceived.

What do I mean by real or perceived? A person may not be intending to harm you but if your mind (perception) is that they are deliberately trying to hurt you, you will suffer a loss because of it. Some people imagine every life setback and problem is God or some other hidden force trying to inflict pain on them. This creates more loss than for another person who has less of a belief in malicious intent.

Babies below the age of two or three do not have the capacity to analyze events as random. By random, I mean no one intended for this to happen. So even though as an adult you recognize an event early on, like a parent who died or who was mentally ill had nothing to do with you, it is still necessary to recapture the perspective of how you experienced the trauma. Therefore, wounding from the womb or early years can only be resolved by recognizing the perception of that time and what losses resulted from that perception.

Though our losses come in all different shapes and sizes, they generally fall into one of four major areas of pain[30]:

---

[30] I first heard this concept explained by Dr. Mario Rivera.

1. Physical pain
2. Social pain
3. Emotional pain
4. Spiritual pain

In each category, the level of pain varies depending on circumstantial factors.

Physical pain is the simplest (though by no means easiest) type of pain. It results from a loss of comfort in the body: the greater the loss of comfort, the greater the pain. Sometimes physical pain can bring to the surface other types of pain as it erodes our ability to keep other losses at bay.

Social pain results from a loss of acceptance. When God created us, He said, "It is not good for man to be alone".[31] He understands our need for belonging. If we are not accepted in social circles –our family, church, school, or the business world—we suffer social loss and experience social pain. This pain varies in degree to the relevance the circles hold in our lives.

A woman I know went to school every day as a child expecting to be spit on and ridiculed. The taunting words and unkind gestures of her schoolmates created manifold losses in her young life. Her constant fear at school threw her into a defensive posture and paranoia that deeply affected her adult relationships.

Such losses are real and need attention even if they were created by your perceptions. If you felt like the black sheep of your family, your pain hurts even if others didn't see it the same way. I grew up in a home where I was the only introvert among a family of extroverts. Because I couldn't relate to the interests of those around me, I felt as if I didn't belong. Because I didn't think that anyone attempted to understand me or share my interests, I felt excluded. If you had questioned others in my family, they would have probably been shocked to hear I felt that way. Though these perceptions

---

[31] Genesis 2:18.

may have exceeded what I experienced, my social loss, nonetheless, stemmed from how I interpreted *reality*.

Social pain diminishes in intensity as the group to which we long to belong increases in size. Suffering a breach in our nuclear family creates the greatest social loss. The pain remains substantial if shunned from our extended family. It continues as a factor in the realm of our town, state, and country.
Some of my clients over the years have experienced the pain of racism. Even hearing about others who are victimized because of their race can create loss. My father came to the United States in the 1920's from Italy and was persecuted and ostracized. Social pain on a national level can be debilitating.

Social pain also afflicts the person who feels embarrassed about his socio-economic status—that others look better, have nicer clothes or cars, more prestigious jobs, etc. Standing before a group of people and not knowing what to say, feeling the lack and resulting shame, are examples of social pain.

The next level of loss is in the emotional and psychological realm. We encounter this pain in our one-on-one relationships with "significant others." Emotional pain involves the loss of feeling loved or safe. Premier examples include death and divorce—the actual loss of the physical presence of a significant other. Any degree of disruption of these relationships due to sickness, travel, practical needs, or emotional unavailability creates emotional loss. Losing a close friend or a group you associated with are also examples of this type of loss.

I work with many people whose parents got divorced after all the children left home. On the surface, it appears they need to address the pain of the divorce. But what emerges quickly is that before the divorce, the lack of harmony in the home was there for many years. This created emotional and psychological losses needing attention as well.

A family is meant to be a haven, a place where we can feel secure. If discord threatens the relationships that create our "safe" environment, then it threatens us. The loss of a safe emotional environment causes emotional pain. We see this most visibly with children. Parents who constantly argue cause a tenuous and mounting sense of emotional loss for their children. Parents' relationships to their children are vital, but psychologists have determined that mom and dad's relationships to each other have even greater influence on their offspring. What the child witnesses transpiring between his parents becomes coded inside as the way to relate to himself.

Jesus said, "Unless you turn and become like a little child you cannot enter the kingdom of heaven."[32] One of the characteristics of small children is their openness to being loved. They are welcoming and receptive to relationship and love. Jesus warned against causing these little ones to sin.

Children learn to stop being open to love when they are hurt in their vulnerable state. Without wanting to, their parents teach them that love is when someone gets close enough to do some serious damage to the most vulnerable parts of the soul.

Unfortunately, I am speaking from experience here with my own four children. I have grieved over my lack of sensitivity to them. I remember how open they were to love me and receiving my love. I wasted many opportunities in their early years to communicate love to them.

Over the years, they became more cautious and guarded about letting me get close. All I could do was to pray for them that God would open the gates of their hearts to His love as the perfect parent I could never be. I had to ask them to forgive me for my failings and encouraged them to grieve these losses so they could find God in their wounding.

I couldn't go back and repair the damage I'd done, but my apology helped them to resolve some of these things before they passed them on to their children. At this point, having their own children has helped our relationship

---

[32] See Matthew 18.

in that now they understand better than ever before the difficulty of always doing the best for your children.

Of all the types of pain to discuss, we find it easiest to talk about physical pain. Therefore, in church circles, we hear more prayer requests for physical ailments than anything else. Social pain requires a little more vulnerability—*No, I didn't have very many friends as a child... I didn't feel like I fit in... I was overweight and I talked too much.*

Our difficulty to authentically communicate our losses rises with the intensity of pain we experience. Emotional pain demands yet more vulnerability to express than social. Rare is the church group where people feel safe enough to share about family abuses and neglect. The tragedy of this lies in the disconnected nature of most congregations.

For many, the church becomes the new family. But with a heart full of unresolved patterns and conflicts ("the empty way of life passed on from our ancestors"[33]), this new family begins to look like the old one. Carrying around preconceived notions about others based on our ungrieved losses[34] makes for rocky and often short relationships. Some persevere and stay in their church, many continue their pilgrimage for the "perfect" church, which, as we know, does not exist.

Spiritual pain is the most profound of all. Spiritual pain, a response to the loss of harmony or communion with God, harms us more than we recognize. We suffer spiritual loss more severely than any other loss because of its supreme and twofold nature. Not only do we need the One who created us more than we need our mother or father, home, reputation, or physical health, but He also is the source of all our provisions. Spiritual loss lies at the root of all loss. If it hadn't been for sin, no pain would have tainted our lives. Separation from God has cost us all, beginning at conception and weaving a web of losses through every area of our life and times.

---

[33] I Peter 1:18.

[34] Later in this book we will take a detailed look at how we keep repeating relationship dramas until our losses are effectively grieved.

Though many of us have been born into a living, active relationship with Jesus at this point of our lives, to some extent, we still confront spiritual loss every day. If, while back in Eden, we had not suffered a loss of harmony with God—if we hadn't fallen away from Him through the rebellion of sin—pain would not exist. All pain results from sin which is separation from God.

Pain and loss, death and grief, fade when this world passes away. In this present life, however, sin thrives. Spiritual loss and pervasive grief remain inextricably tied.

Through the prophet, Hosea, the Lord says to us, "In their affliction they will earnestly seek Me" (v. 5:15). Don't misunderstand here. God doesn't do evil, but He does take advantage of the fact that suffering people are more open to what He is trying to offer. Pain can be a vehicle to bring us closer to Himself, to cause us to know God more fully, to understand His ways and to believe His promises for us. As only God can, He uses sin and its consequences—the very things that cause and define our separation from Him—to draw us to Himself.

From God's perspective, the goal of our pain is the restoration of our spiritual loss. Here, too, the converse is worth stating—addressing our spiritual loss through a greater intimacy with God makes it more likely that we can face our other losses. Christ is the remedy to the loss and pain of the human condition. "(*He is*) the Father of mercies and the God of *all* comfort... who comforts us in *all* our afflictions."[35]

Speaking of God like this may mean very little to you if you have never had encounters with Him to discover His true character. Hopefully reading this book will open your heart to consider He may not be as you have imagined Him. If we have positive and loving encounters with other people, this can help us to deal with all the different types of losses we have experienced. The family and the church were designed to be such "groups" but where

---

[35] 2 Corinthians 1:4

they have not fulfilled this role, other types of support groups have stepped in to fill the gap.

Now that we have laid out the different types of losses requiring grieving, next we want to look at the prerequisites necessary for this natural process of grief to unfold and leave us more fully alive. In our next chapter, we address the result of feeling safe which is the ability to be vulnerable.

Chapter 6—Vulnerability

Have you ever thought about how vulnerable babies are? They have no choice but to lie about hoping someone will come meet their basic needs and want them. We all began like that, without exception. Over the years we turn away from such vulnerability and become hardened. This is understandable. But to grieve, something must happen to reverse this hardening process and open us up again to that child-like part of the soul.

To return to your child-like vulnerability, you will need a safe place. It may be a loving person or group. It may be a time in your life when you don't have much pressure, or it may come from a connection with God. But before you can unpack the pain and loss, you must be convinced you can be vulnerable and not get destroyed.

Often, there are layers of negative responses piled inside, inhibiting vulnerability and, therefore, grief. Resentment about people or circumstances, past and present, can block access to our child-like nature. In our counseling practice, my co-worker, Richard Kinney, and I rarely find a person who doesn't have resentment right below the surface. It may even be directed at God though rarely do people easily admit it.

This was certainly true of my life when I returned from 7 years on the mission field. I could not admit any of it. Quite simply, I was not authentic and was unable to be vulnerable. I had never been safe with anyone and I could not be safe with God. Intellectually, I knew truth, but I hadn't fully experienced it. In some areas of my life, it never penetrated.

"Yes, yes, God is wonderful, and I am in a new family and everything the Bible says is true." I said one thing, but in my heart, I believed another. Unfortunately, no matter how many times I said that I wanted to believe (what I recognized in my mind as truth), these truths did not touch the parts of me full of resentment and locked in pain.

From the time I accepted Christ, I assumed that I could decide to believe what I wanted. I then proceeded to build my Christian life *by deciding* to replace my quasi-truths, with His. It was mental: neat, quick, clean, and relatively painless. I was painting fresh coats of paint on rotting wood.

I had great theory with little hope of living it out in practice. "Jesus was a man of sorrows, acquainted with grief." Knowledge did not spare Him the pain of His losses any more than it could spare me. Through grief, Jesus came to resolution. Through no other route than embracing the full range of emotions created by His losses, could He forgive others, which is the last stage of grief. "He learned obedience," Scripture tells us, "from the things He suffered"[36].

Jesus made Himself vulnerable to suffering. Isn't it amazing how He allowed His life to begin as an infant and submitted to parents! He got emotional about the faith of non-Jews, the pain of loss, the "lostness" of the masses, the hunger of those following him, the hypocrisy of the Pharisees. Jesus was that humble, that authentic. The conflicts that plagued my soul could only be addressed in following His way: being a person of sorrow and acquainted with grief, living authentically and being vulnerable. Acquainting ourselves with grief doesn't mean we stay there: it is an avenue to becoming a conqueror over the losses of your life. Resurrection life power follows the cross of grieving.

Once of the greatest pictures in Scripture of Jesus requiring his followers to be vulnerable is at the Last Supper. He asks to wash their feet, our feet. This is where we submit to Him seeing, touching and washing all those things we have walked through willingly or unwillingly. He cleanses us of the ruin and mess they have left upon us. Grieving is a cleansing progress, a healing process. Without it we carry unhealthy, germy grime which sickens our souls.

---

[36]Hebrews 5:7.

There was a great irony in me using my work as a missionary to distract me from the issues of my heart. I believed God was much more interested in my service than my soul's transformation or my ability to bond with Him. In my relationship with God, I was making a "triangle" out of me, God and mission. He and I related through our mutual interest in getting people saved as far as I was concerned.

Some people relate to Him through various issues or causes: intercessory prayer, Israel, freeing people caught in sex trafficking, service to the poor, social or political causes, worship, to name a few. Others are caught up in the latest doomsday prophecy or fear-mongering descriptions of demons and witches.

Everyone relates to others through triangles. A triangle has three points. You are one point; the other person is the second point and whatever you both focus on as a way of connection makes the third point. This is normal and healthy and the usual way we meet someone. We attend the same church or support group. Our kids play softball together. We serve on the same board. We fight for a particular cause, etc. But making ourselves vulnerable happens when we grow safe enough in intimacy to drop the third point of the triangle and connect one-on-one to another person—or God.

But most relationships never reach the stage of moving past the triangle. We may use our triangles to stay at a distance and never have to share our hearts. One-on-one intimacy is replaced by a shared interest, life circumstance, problem or person. Married couples who only relate through the care of the children can find little reason to stay together when the last child leaves home. We can attend a church for years and be involved in many of its activities only to discover we have never made a friend. That would require connecting one-to-one without a reason for it other than to simply get acquainted with one another. Sometimes that can happen in the course of triangling, but it requires intentionality and vulnerability on our part.

You can busy your life with activities so that there is never a silent pause where you experience intimacy with yourself and peek at what losses and pain may be there needing to be grieved. You can avoid intimacy with God and other people by never connecting to your own heart.

Being around small children will offer us an education in how to be vulnerable, authentic, how to connect with another person and how to grieve. They approach us with no expectation that we don't want to be with them or get to know them. If things are not going well, notice how they grieve spontaneously. They might have a toy, for instance, and if that toy is taken from them, their first response is one of shock. Then they become angry, they start to cry, and they fight to try to take it back. If they can't get it back by force, they will likely cry for a while then return and plead for the toy. If this bears no fruit, they eventually give up and move on to something else. That's the grieving process in a nutshell—shock, anger, sadness, bargaining and resolution. It's automatic. No one needs to instruct them. No one needs to say, "Okay, now it's time to move from anger to sadness."

If a child experiences a loss, however, and doesn't have a safe place to grieve, the grieving must wait. Sanctuary, a safe place where we feel safe and accepted, is a prerequisite for vulnerability. Without it, the child will shut down and stay in the first stage of grief: shock/denial. More than likely, the child will recall his loss on an intellectual level, but his emotions will deny that anything has happened. If denial of loss is practiced on a regular basis, there will be a split in the child. Thinking will go one way and emotions will go another.

Once safe enough[37], the child's loss will resurface, bringing with it the natural emotional response of the grieving process. As the child grieves, his loss heals, and any false beliefs associated with it disintegrate along with the pain that created them.

A friend of mine adopted a little girl as an infant. Before the adoption was final, the infant was given back to the mother temporarily and then permanently placed in my friend's home. One day, a few years after the

_____

[37] Which may not happen until much later in life.

33

adoption was finalized, this four-year-old child was watching an animal show on TV. During the show, she saw a wild animal with a litter of babies. For some reason, the babies were to be taken from the mother. At this point in the show, this small child became extremely agitated and upset. She ran to my friend and clung to her shirt crying, "Don't let them take the babies away from the mommy!" Repeatedly she screamed this pitiful phrase.

My friends loving care had provided the sanctuary necessary for the little girl to be vulnerable and begin to grieve. Also, fortunately, my friend had been taught something about the grieving process. She held the child close and reassured her that the babies would be fine. When the child had been quieted, my friend explained the story of her adoption. The child sat and absorbed this information, connecting her fear that had been stirred by the TV show to the fact of her own life. The truth was spoken in love to her fearful heart and she had peace at the end of her grieving. This simple but powerful moment with her adoptive mother will help to prevent great anxiety later in her life. A few safe moments with someone who cares to be vulnerable and grieve part of a loss: the world suffers constantly for lack of such sanctuary.

Make no mistake, though, until the time comes when a person feels safe enough to be vulnerable, the loss waits, the emotions wait, the healing waits. Later, in Part 2, we will demonstrate how life events that display any similarity to the hidden trauma can cause a perplexing over-reaction to current life situations.

It's not uncommon for children to reach adulthood still in a state of shock from losses in youth. The little girl mentioned above was "triggered" by something she saw. You may be triggered daily to remember your losses. But because you don't recognize your unresolved grief, you gloss over them.

We have distracted ourselves from considering we may be the problem that needs to be solved. We may blame others and ignore the intensity of our reactions. Or we may suppress our emotions and hurry to say we have forgiven. Especially as Christians, we feel obliged to jump from offense to forgiveness in a single bound. That's the honorable thing, right? But "forgiveness" without sounding out the loss, pain and its significance leaves little to forgive.

As adults, we rationalize, "Well, you know, Dad had a hard life. Mom was preoccupied. She had to work all the time." We push down the emotions from these losses, careful not to be vulnerable and feel, continuing to pretend that any pain ever existed. The problem is, though, that it did. Somewhere within us, it still does. No amount of mental gymnastics can rewrite our history.

It's not that our parents were so bad. They may have been quite exceptional for parents. The problem is that God is SO GOOD. And His perfect unconditional love is what our hearts were created for. Anything less leaves us with loss and pain that needs to be grieved. The more our parents modeled God's parenting, the less loss we will suffer, and the less we will have to grieve.

As hard as you may work to suppress unwanted emotions, they fight to emerge. You can exhaust yourself struggling with them daily through the course of your life. Somehow, though, you can be oblivious to the source of your exhaustion, blinded to the cause of your depression. You can easily blame others for your chronic anger and discontent, or for the repeated failures of broken relationships. Some people turn the bitterness and resentment on themselves and live in a toxic internal environment of self-loathing.

Are we safe enough to make our hearts vulnerable to truth? The Bible tells us that God's Word is "truth"[38]. Not only that, but His word is "living and active and sharper than any two-edged sword and piercing as far as the division of soul and spirit"[39]. We're promised that "the truth shall set *(us)* free".[40] We must understand, though, that we will only know God's truths at the levels we experience them. If we stay in our heads—merely believing

---

[38] John. 17:17.
[39] Hebrews 4:2.
[40] John. 8:32.

but not receiving—our intellects may indeed receive freedom, but the rest of us will remain in confusion and fear.

A lack of vulnerability and constant triangling will leave us unable to receive love (from God and others) and to give love, particularly to those closest to us such as our spouses and children.

Besides needing a safe place to be vulnerable in order to grieve, we also need to resolve the contradictory feelings we have towards those who have created the losses in our lives.

When people or situations produce loss for us, it's typical to experience ambivalent feelings. Ambivalence is when we have two contradictory feelings at the same time. Love and hate can be very close. We will often hate someone whom we needed so much and who let us down. The hate arises from the disappointment of love.

For children, these contradictory feelings appear irreconcilable. Unable to resolve ambivalence, they often decide to *make* a parent all "good" or all "bad". Their inability to acknowledge strengths and weaknesses residing side-by-side in one person causes them to record their past incorrectly.

Many adults, as well, struggle in integrating the "good" and "bad" within others. We can idealize (or demonize) friends, spouses, siblings, and parents. If we idealize them, it is difficult to admit they have hurt us. Truly, only God is completely good. Everyone else will somehow disappoint us and betray us eventually, even if it is simply by dying! If we are honest, the further we advance in life the more we will recognize that no other person can give us everything we long for.

Everyone in our lives is a bad person capable of good things and a good person capable of bad things. Refusing to accept the humanness of ourselves and others leaves us divorced from reality and unable to grieve effectively. To find restoration through the grieving process, we must break through the barrier of ambivalence.

Our deepest beliefs about God need to surface so we can resolve our ambivalent feelings about Him as well. Is He really good? Does He really care?

We need to feel safe enough to say, *I feel a sense of loss, Lord, because I'm not 100% sure You want to take care of me. I had believed that my parents were gods, and I thought if only they would (fill in the blank) that I would be happy. I now realize that they were only human, and they couldn't. But You truly are God. You can! All along, You could! So, why didn't You?*

If we resist acknowledging these emotions, we exclude God from answering the questions they raise. If we answer them ourselves, but not with truth, we will not heal our loss. Instead, our false beliefs lay hidden from the light, and block our access to God's help.

Resolving ambivalence by facing truth and choosing to be vulnerable again allows the innate ability to grieve inside of us to evolve. Our eyes begin to open, and we can finally face our internal reality. This is where we pick up in our next chapter.

Chapter 7—Facing the Truth We Carry

No one needs to teach us to grieve, God put "code" inside us. As we have already stated, we need safety to grieve. Along with our sincerity, we must have a non-condemning place to be vulnerable and honest. Love has to buffer us on each side so the truth can pull down barriers to the grieving process. Love helps to usher in the fulfillment of God's promise, "the truth shall set you free".

We all need a safe place to have good grief. Confession in its truest form needs to take place again and again. For example, you need to express your anger towards a distant and cold father but eventually you will need to weep over any way you have done the same thing to your children and loved ones.

At the end of the process of grief, we come to understand if the parent who hurt us was once a victim, too. The hearts of the fathers turn towards the children and the hearts of the children towards the fathers.[41] True reconciliation and forgiveness come only after losses from evil are sounded out and embraced.

Jesus spoke in John 16 of how his disciples would grieve but by their next encounter with Him, their grief would be turned to joy. That is the pattern we will follow as we grieve. The end of the road is to feel good again because God has restored our soul and brought us to a place of rest in Him. We come out stronger and more resilient and less thrown about by life circumstances. Our problem-solving skills improve because we have a track record of hope.

I used to think I was very tough and strong before good grief came into my life. I saw myself as being hard and able to bounce off whatever life dealt me. As good grief came into my life, I saw that it was this very same attitude in my mother that hurt me deeply. She seemed impervious to me, my needs, and my suffering as a child.

---

[41] Malachi 3.

The first step was to recognize the losses I suffered as a result of her hardness. Admitting my same hardness was step two. Facing the effects of my own coldness towards my children came next. Finally, I could conclude that I understood my mother and why she acted the way she did: it had been done to her as well. Forgiveness of my mother was possible—sincere and deep. My heart turned to her. My heart turned to my children. Healing would be possible, and the generational curse of hardness could be broken.

Shakespeare said "Give sorrow words. The grief that does not speak, whispers the o'erfraught heart, and bids it break." If we were to map out our lives on a timeline and mark when we came to know God, we would see a visual picture of all the points before that time when we lived unaware of His presence. God wants to meet us in every place where we did not encounter His love. He desires to give Himself to us. In every disappointment, every cause of bitterness or resentment. He wants to soothe us and become the fulfillment of what we did not receive from this world. He wants to help us grieve so that we can become whole and fully bonded to Him. Knowing we are enjoyed and wanted gives us an internal strength and joy independent of circumstances.

The person most interested in our healing is the Holy Spirit. Jesus said, "But the Comforter, the Holy Spirit, whom the Father will send in My name, He will teach you all things, and bring to your remembrance all that I said to you"[42]. The Holy Spirit takes up residence inside of us once we accept Christ. He works 24 hours a day, seven days a week to bring fullness to our lives. If there are rooms of unresolved grief, negative emotions and unforgiveness within us, He will lovingly and persistently offer to help us clean them out through encouragement, unconditional love, discipline and, of course, the grieving process. As we cooperate with the Holy Spirit, our lives will become quite an adventure with plenty of healing, satisfaction and good fruit.

And the Holy Spirit's purpose in this work in our soul is to bring us into a greater ease, freedom and enjoyment of being all that God created us to be.

---

[42] John 14:17, 26.

It has nothing to do with making us more valuable or worthy or able to be loved. We are not earning love through the healing process; we are simply becoming more capable of receiving the vast supply of it already existing for us!

Some people, in their evangelistic zeal cry, "We need to forget about ourselves and get on with going to the nations." Wisdom says believers need to give out of that which they have received. Too many times the church has taken people who still see themselves as orphans (someone needing to perform to have worth) and shipped them off to do battle. Should we send our crippled and diseased troops who will reproduce converts modeled after their broken and love-less lives? Having been a missionary, I know this too well.

I did not begin to address the massive losses of my life until I was thirty-three. When the Lord led me to begin addressing them, I felt overwhelmed. Many hurts and losses surfaced, some taking me months to grieve completely. Some I grieved in a matter of a day. In the beginning, though, emotions of anger and hatred seemed to overtake me.

I would wake up in the morning saying, *Ooo... I hate... I hate!* It wasn't something I invented at that moment. Years of vintage anger had surfaced, unassisted, from this deep emotional well buried within me. For the first time in my life, I felt safe enough to release them and give them expression. The Lord had convinced me—and *convicted* me—that those who "worship Him must worship in spirit and truth"[43]. This demanded that I honestly grieve my losses. In those days, if I was authentic with God, it would have to start right where I was. I had recently come out of denial about my losses and that left me facing huge anger that had been pressed down for many years.

Think about it: Did God know my emotions existed? Yes. Did I? Not really. All the while I pushed them down, stiffening to suppress them; I had become increasingly hard and unreachable. I separated myself from myself,

---

[43] John 4:24.

and wasn't truly available for Him, or anyone for that matter. Worst of all, I did this and didn't really know I was doing it. And to the extent that I did realize that I was burying my emotions, I believed I was doing it in obedience to God. My heart had me fooled about myself.

I mentioned that I was ministering in North Africa. My undoing began when I was confronted by my strong reaction of anger towards Arab men. The culture of North Africa, at that time, was very demeaning and dishonoring of women. Females were treated as second-class citizens with limited rights.

Women were degraded in my own family. I remember how when someone had a baby and we heard "It's a girl.", my father's Italian family would reply, "That's too bad." I am not kidding! Also, the sexuality of women was portrayed as such: women were not allowed to have a normal or healthy sexuality but were supposed to be asexual—and if they did show signs of being sexual then they were whores.

I had never faced my family's belief system or admitted my anger resulting from it. This anger poisoned my ministry and prevented me from sincerely loving men who reminded me of past abusers. But for years I didn't even know why I was angry. No amount of repenting or denying my anger made it go away. It was only by linking it to its point of origination in my original family that allowed me to grieve it. And it was only by grieving it that I could be released from it and be open to receive God's perspective about women, restoring and setting me free.

I was in shock most of my life about the emotional, physical and sexual abuse that went on in my family. For me it was normal. I remember asking my husband one day, "If someone was hit in the head back and forth and pulled out of bed by the hair, would that be considered physical abuse?" Gary looked at me like I was joking and said, "Of course." I could never remember feeling the pain of the beatings. I remembered the shame of the rejection but had no memories connected to the physical pain. My body seemed to belong to someone else. It has taken me many years to reconnect to my body and the pain. It helped me greatly to know that Jesus understood physical beatings and wouldn't run from me when I confessed how awful it was. Admitting it hurt was the first step to healing.

When we confront our loss, even in this numb, detached state, the grieving process begins. It proceeds to anger, sadness, bargaining and, finally, forgiveness and resolution. Now we will look at the stages of grief in more detail.

Chapter 8—The Process of Grief

First Stage of Grief—Shock[44]

Shock is a natural response to pain and injury. In the moment of crisis, shock buffers us. Though reflex-like, shock is the body's way of protecting itself, a way of staying in ultimate control. Our pain is held at bay. Once we feel safe enough to be vulnerable, we automatically begin the grieving process and start to relinquish this control. With each of the subsequent stages, we surrender a level of control in exchange for a level of pain. In this, God ensures that our emotions will not overwhelm us.

Disassociation [45]is a mental defense mechanism, like shock in the physical realm, which allows us to avoid mental pain and trauma. Disassociation can create the sense that we are detached from the suffering and observing the suffering of someone else. Unlike physical shock, which eventually dissipates after the injury occurs, it is possible to stay in a perpetual state of disassociation to avoid emotional pain. It is only when we can face our loss (i.e. becoming relationally safe) that our emotional shock will give way to anger.

A man came to me for help who had been adopted. He would joke about being left on the doorstep of a church. He couldn't admit that the abandonment by his parents had affected him. His reason for seeking help was that his second marriage was falling apart, and he didn't want another divorce. It took some time, but he eventually came to see that although he had denied his anger and resentment toward his parents, he was now directing a disproportionate amount of anger at his wife and driving her away from him.

Second stage–Anger

---

[44] The Kübler-Ross model, commonly known as the five stages of grief, was first introduced by Elisabeth Kübler-Ross in her 1969 book, On Death and Dying.
[45] This is the feeling that we are watching what is happening to us rather than experiencing it.

Imagine for a minute that we witness a mother screaming at her four-year-old child. *"You are so stupid! You spilled your milk! I should make you get down and lick that up like the dog that you are!"* How should we react to that scenario? Would it be normal to calmly defend the mother by stating that she probably was having an "off" day or didn't know any better... that perhaps she had "personal issues" which depleted her ability to cope? Honestly, is there a good reason to justify her behavior? On the contrary, something would be terribly wrong with us if that situation didn't cause us anger.

When we emerge from shock, anger naturally follows. We finally come to face our loss at a deeper level. Anger has an appropriate place as part of the grieving process. Anger clouds the mind but uncovers the heart.[46] Touching the original anger of a wounding creates a moment of authenticity where we can own ourselves and move forward from that place. Ironically, if we experience anger as part of grieving, we won't stay angry but will move on to the next stage of grief. But if we deny it, we stay stuck and may become depressed or find ourselves raging at those around us in an inappropriate way or, even worse, become passive-aggressive where we secretly beat up everyone with our negativity and ineffectiveness.

Anger marks a milestone on our God-ordained progression towards healing. Many of us shudder and flee at the slightest display of anger. *Christians aren't supposed to feel angry,* a voice in our head whispers. But who said? Doesn't God Himself experience anger over the acts and consequences of sin?

What about a child who's made to sit on the stairs from ten o'clock in the morning till six at night waiting for her father to come home to beat her?[47] Or how about a boy whose father disciplines him by crushing his bare toes under the weight of his work boots? Shouldn't we feel angry with something

---

[46] My early mentor, Dr. Mario Rivera, used to say this.
[47] Years ago, I ministered to a woman who experienced such abuse in her early life.

like that? Why, then, when wounded souls such as these finally come out of denial should we expect instant forgiveness without any emotion?

A subtler but equally insidious sin against children is common in Christian families. The hidden justification for abuse goes something like this:

The way others perceive us as a family, and us as parents, is VERY important. The way you act when others are looking is far more important than how you feel or what you think. Wear a mask that protects our reputation as parents because this is valued more highly than who you are what your vision may be for yourself or the problems you might have.

Without a word, it is possible to communicate this deadly message to children by various non-verbal signals and reactions. Pretending this is not evil denies truth. God indeed judges the heart. But parents may rarely take the time to listen to what is in the heart of a child. Instead they insist that children perform certain behaviors refusing to recognize the child's viewpoint.

Touching anger at being treated as a non-person in the family system can be tough because it is neglect rather than abuse. Sometimes it will dawn on you gradually how you came away from your "family" experience feeling uncomfortable about just being you—like you somehow missed the memo on how to feel positive and happy about yourself.

I remember when my youngest was in kindergarten. One day he didn't want to go. I held him in my arms while he cried about having to go and expressed why he wanted to stay home. I comforted him in his sorrow but still made him go to school. He didn't get his way, but he knew his sadness and anger were acceptable ways to express loss. Isn't God willing to listen to our anger and sadness tirelessly in prayer, affirming our feelings but still doing what is best for us?

There are times when being angry at something happening to you or around you is perfectly valid. When people or organizations twist the truth and tell lies, we shouldn't be sitting around turning the other cheek. We need to stand for truth. Jesus confronted and challenged people promoting lies. There were times when He didn't defend himself and other times when He went after his accusers with vehemence.

By and large I believe Christians have much more of a problem refusing to get openly angry because of their fear of what people may think rather than because they are holy and turning the other cheek. People may view themselves as "godly" for their lack of response but often it is simply a mixture of cowardice, apathy and complacency.

"Be angry, and sin not," Scripture tells us[48]. So, we know there are valid expressions of anger—we are not meant to carry it around all the time. Inflammation in the body is helpful if it is fighting a germ or healing a wound. But chronic inflammation is debilitating. Anger is a good choice to bring modification or changes in the short haul but allowing it to linger, fester and burry itself in our soul will take a toll on our well-being and open us up to footholds of the enemy.

Without question, it is sinful to hurt someone, physically or verbally, to be vengeful, inconsiderate or malicious. Anger is usually associated with hurting others. The person expressing the anger feels temporarily relieved and diffused, but they have caused physical, emotional, or financial loss to others. That is not the way to be angry and sin not. One way of being angry and not sinning is in our response to grief.

We can
- Direct our present-day anger to its root cause
- Express our anger in a way that will not hurt ourselves or others
- Correct the belief system from which the anger stems.

Let me explain this process with an example: a woman told me this story. Her four-year-old daughter spilled some rice on the kitchen floor. The mother, who had just cleaned up the kitchen, became emotional and angry. She scolded the child for her "thoughtlessness" and banished her to her

---

[48] Ephesians 4:26.

room. The mother was perplexed about her strong reaction to such a minor, unintentional accident.

We discussed the incident and her reaction to her daughter. Her anger was triggered by the deeply held, hidden belief that children are not deserving of understanding and consideration, as well as the right to express feelings. Her own mother had taught her this. She had never been allowed to be angry with her own mother but now she had the opportunity to express her emotions freely towards her daughter. She was demanding her daughter give her the help and consideration she never felt she had received from her own mother long ago.

When this dear woman saw how she was unfairly dumping anger on her little one, she cried. I led her through an exercise where she admitted all that she had wanted from her mother, what she lost from never having received it and then agreeing to forgive her mother and seek the compassion and understanding she craved from a relationship with God in Christ Jesus.

There may be a wounded child in you beneath the surface. When something happens in your present life that steps on the emotional I.O.U.'s of that child, you will insist on payment from others, blaming them for your anger and pain until you recognize your losses and their roots. With good grief, you can resolve those losses and have God take over where others have failed you.

It leads to sin to deny your hurt. If you deny it, your pain remains unexpressed, buried, and dormant. It can be reactivated by some event that causes you to remember to some degree the original pain. You may not actually remember the event, but your memory, and original pain, is triggered, which then activates a whole series of emotions.

As I stated earlier, you may sometimes erupt like a volcano or shoot off like a loose cannon at your children, friends, co-workers or spouse. Or even worse, you may completely lose awareness of your anger. A passive-aggressive reaction is where you secretly release your unconscious hostility by tardiness, sloppiness, convenient forgetfulness, and side-handed ways to consistently convey anger towards everyone triggering your original pain. Cynicism and sarcasm are disguised expressions of anger. Some of the funny people you know who have a little jab for everyone, may be angry but unable to deal with it directly.

It's far more constructive for a person to stamp their feet, let out a few bad words, yell and holler and admit they're angry than to behave like a Pharisee who essentially said, *I'm not angry, but I'll find a way to get back at you.* The Pharisees were full of passive-aggressive anger. They would never admit to Jesus: *You are threatening our political structure. We're angry with You because You look more important than us.*

Perhaps it would have been their salvation to admit they were angry. Instead they said, *No, no, no, we're not angry. But let's just have a little meeting to see what we can do to rid ourselves of Him.* Being cold, unreachable and calculating are further ways to be angry without looking angry. The Pharisees couldn't receive the One they had been waiting for, the Messiah, because of their refusal to admit the anger in their hearts. How about us? Will repressed anger hinder us from fully knowing our God?

Third stage–Sadness

Sadness is the flip side of anger. Remember that each stage of grief leads to a greater powerlessness and a greater letting go of what was lost. Sadness is more powerless than anger, closer to a full acceptance of loss. Sadness is simply, letting it hurt. Where anger causes you to feel powerful and somehow able to bring change, sadness is a relaxing of the fist. It is a sore and tender place of self-inventory. After being angry over childhood abuse and neglect, a wounded person will move on in the grieving process when they finally stop fighting the past and embrace the tragedy of being overpowered and used or forgotten.

One woman told me. "I have kept alive by staying angry. If I let myself cry, I may never stop. Somehow that seems like a defeat. To be so weak would be like dying."

Her wounded soul was locked in a standoff. Her will to survive fought with her need for good grief. When she finally felt safe with me, the tears came. Her anger vanished and a well of sorrow replaced it. A side effect of her grieving these losses was the disappearance of chronic headaches that had plagued her for years.

Some add another stage of grief here: depression. It is a short lived, non-clinical depression. I believe it is the first confession of powerlessness on the way to forgiveness. Ultimate forgiveness can only come when we have stopped fighting off the loss and embraced the consequences of what has occurred. In short, it is learning to deal with reality.

I suffered clinical depression for many years. I was on medications. I used special lamps to try and raise the serotonin levels in my brain. I exercised, engaged in positive thinking, memorized Scripture, etc. Every month someone had another bright idea of how I could raise myself out of my depression. But there was no remedy for it.

When I started grieving, the depression finally began to lift over time. For each loss that fueled my depression, I had to come out of denial. I touched the anger and sadness. Then I would usually suffer a few days of depression. But this depression was different. Instead of feeling like I was holding back a dam, it was a depression from an inner relinquishment of control. I had lost the battle to avoid pain. It hurt but there was hope in it.

The past cannot be changed. But our timeless God can come and be with us[49] in the part of our souls injured by the loss. This is the practical outworking of these two promises in Scripture:

"Jesus Christ is the same yesterday, today and forever."[50]

And

---

[49] See Richard Kinney's "Stepping Into Freedom From Pain" at firehouseministries.com to help you do this healing exercise.
[50] Hebrews 13

"He restores my soul."[51]

It turns evil to good as you let go of your own solution and coping mechanisms and welcome the Presence of Jesus Christ instead. The depression in true grief is a critical turning point as you approach true forgiveness. Think of David when he wrote the verses, "though my mother and father forsake me, you will receive me". Did he have some depression as he contemplated the opinion his parents had of him? Or when he experienced God's love for him in his mother's womb[52], was he having healing from some loss from that hidden time of his life?

Fourth stage–Bargaining

The next stage, bargaining, is a place where the will makes a last-ditch effort to alleviate the suffering of losses. *Do I really have to accept this? Can't I work it out another way?* I believe the deepest "deal" in all our hearts involves control and performance. *Surely there must be some way to make people love me. I will be acceptable by doing better.*

A man, Stan, who received ministry from me, kept on trying to get his father to understand him. He played out this drama in job after job with his bosses. Later, he set up a meeting with his dad in the hopes they could finally have the "heart to heart" talk he longed for. But his father had made it clear repeatedly that he was not interested in discussing their relationship.

Stan grieved many losses concerning his father. For a period, he kept on returning to the same place. He kept trying to communicate his need to his father in a way in which his father would finally respond. He begged, he demanded, he reasoned, he challenged his father, but to no avail. Finally, he had to admit that he was beaten. He could never get the understanding out of Dad he longed for. Eventually he let it go, finished his grief, and forgave his father. The result was that he accepted his Dad just as he was, and their relationship improved!

---

[51] Psalm 23.
[52] Psalm 139

50

In his book, *Inside Out*, Larry Crab mentions the tendency to heap contempt on others or on ourselves rather than accepting that only God is enough. Bargaining says: *I'll make it happen by being smarter, thinner, more loving, more spiritual* ... you fill in the blank. Demanding the impossible from ourselves or others never resolves a thing. It sets you up for disappointment and resentments that weaken relationships.

Often the spouse of an unfaithful partner knows the excruciating bargaining that follows oscillating episodes of rage and sorrow. *We'll make this marriage work by having another baby. It was just a fling. Our marriage is just fine. What could I have done differently?*

If you persist in trying to bargain away pain, you settle into deceit, or magical thinking. just like in fairy tales, you create in your mind an imaginary world. Like in all the stages of grief, when you refuse to embrace the pain and loss, you get stuck. Delayed grief can cause you many problems which we will discuss in further depth later. Again, at this stage, only by God's grace can we accept the truth and move towards the freedom of forgiveness. "You will know the truth and the truth will set you free"[53].

Final stage–Resolution/Forgiveness

Matthew 18:35 warns that our sins will not be forgiven, "...unless you forgive your brother **from your heart**." As stated earlier, we cannot do things in our minds and leave the rest of us untouched. That is forgiveness in name only. What is wrong with forgiving superficially? A lot. For one, if our forgiveness is superficial, we haven't let go of our anger and are still holding on to our loss. Secondly, we are deceived into thinking that the issue is forgiven and behind us. Forgiving from the heart, as we know, is not an easy matter. It is painful. It requires that we first resurface the original pain. It should not be surprising then that if we won't grieve, we won't be able to forgive from the heart.

---

[53] John 8:32.

Sounding out our loss through our emotions brings us to a clear, truthful state. The emotions are the smoke that leads us to the fire of our most inner belief systems. At first, we need to see the hurt from the eyes of the child within as a matter of authenticity. Once we connect the feeling to the event (abuse, neglect, trauma, etc.), we "re-inhabit" that part of our soul and invite Christ to go there with us and bring us out to a new place of health and safety. We see we are no longer dependent or held captive by those who hurt us. This frees us to think as an adult. The repressed anger and sadness can't cloud our vision like before and we can objectively look at the lives of those who hurt us and possess genuine compassion and understanding. This doesn't diminish what we suffered. But in that place of suffering and grief, in that vulnerable moment of honesty we have opened our hearts to God's manifest presence.

Jesus Christ Himself comes and communes with us in our loss and disappointment. He restores our souls and gives us Himself where we had been clinging to a significant other. Knowing He is there, we can well afford to cancel the debt of those who have hurt and betrayed us. It is here that we move from knowing God in our head to knowing Him in our heart.

Feeling the comfort of God directly in the place where you have been abused or scorned or forgotten is better than life. It is sweeter than the original abuse was bitter. It brings fullness where there was emptiness and companionship where there was loneliness. It causes the emotional cup of your heart to overflow with love.[54]

My friend and co-worker, Richard was deserted by both parents at six months old. His grandparents dutifully raised him, but no one really wanted him. In his forties, he pursued knowing the Father heart of God with the help of a ministry dedicated to that.[55] By the time I met him, he still had many grief issues to address, but there was an unusual strength in his character. It came from a deep-seated embracing of the truth that God had created him and wanted him no matter what his parents did. From there he

---

[54] One resource for learning to feel God's presence more deeply is a workbook by James Wilder called Joyful Journey Listening to Immanuel.

[55] The ministry of Jack Frost.

set on the road to grieve the rest of his losses. The result was healing for his soul and a closer walk with God.

Like many who have been seriously rejected by their parents, his forgiveness of them has been a long process. Hurts that span many years are not quickly or easily grieved. There is a necessary sounding out of all the implications and results of complicated losses. How will we know when the forgiveness is complete? The greatest sign is a welling up of compassion for those who have hurt us. God's ability to forgive becomes a part of us. Our communion with Him feeds our soul, restores it, and causes an overflow.

This then enables our hearts to love others, even those that have hurt us. Now, we are free to forgive, and we can make that decision to forgive with integrity, in full view of the cost. Now our forgiveness will be authentic. It will not be easy, but it will not be superficial. It will reflect our God's agonizing act of forgiveness.

After the resolution of God's anger, seen on the Cross, His relationship with man becomes based on what He can give to us, not what we can give to Him. He no longer demands that we pay a debt we can never pay. When we grieve our losses, we come to the point when we no longer relate to others from the expectation of receiving. We cease to demand that others meet our needs and be what we want them to be for us. Our relationships become balanced between what we can give and what we can receive.

Our giving flows out of the provision we have received of God's presence into the deepest wounding and disappointments of our lives. This is the kind of person who can live out the Sermon on the Mount. One who can, from the heart, bless enemies, turn the other cheek, and give without demanding recognition. These behaviors are not forced imitation but free flowing natural responses from the deepest part of our being.

We have been discussing the benefits and good outcomes of expressing our grief to its completion. But what if we are unwilling or unable to grieve?

What does that cost us? The answer to this question is the subject of our next chapter.

Chapter 9—The Cost of Delayed/Impaired Grief

Do you know that from the moment of creation, you've been a "trust fund baby"? God made a trust fund of His love, for you, not for anybody else, with your name on it; that stretches all the way into eternity. He is determined on you benefiting from that trust fund. That is your destiny and it begins here and now. So, His intention is to guide you in this process of letting go (grieving) all that would block your receiving all the good He has prepared for you.

What happens when a child from a severely deprived background gets adopted into a new loving family? They must learn a whole new set of provisions, expectations and responses based on the change in their lives. An important part of that transformation is a recognition of a new interpretation of what is "normal." This can be a difficult process, but it is the only way to receive all the benefits of the new family system. What makes these changes challenging is that the only way to fully let go of the old ways is to recognize them as losses and grieve those losses. Without a letting go of the old, there is a barrier to receiving the new.

Every child of God is adopted into His new family and has a similar path to travel. If we are not walking in the fullness of all God has promised us in His Word, then it may be because we have not fully released all the "old ways" we had formerly accepted as the norm.

As we have stated earlier, the grieving process will unfold naturally unless something happens to make it stop. The lack of a safe environment mostly aborts grieving. Children from dysfunctional families usually do not grieve their losses during childhood because they don't feel safe enough to express what they're experiencing. They won't even recognize just how awful it is at that time. Once safe, which often isn't until adulthood, grieving will begin.

A friend in college, Jean, grew up with an alcoholic mother. Life with Mom was like living with a time bomb. Nobody knew when the bomb of her mother's rage would explode and injure an unsuspecting victim. Jean never grieved any of her losses. There wasn't room in the family for anyone else's emotions. Mom sucked up all the emotional energy.

The toll of delayed grief in Jean's life emerged in her insecurities and lack of confidence. She had relationships where she often played the role of a helper or an enabler. Fortunately for her, she married someone who was kind and caring.

In the safety of her new home with a kind husband, the pent-up grief in her soul rose to express itself. She told me she spent several days on her couch alternating between rage and tears over the treatment by her mother.

For a couple of months, she didn't speak to her perplexed mother. But after taking the time to get it all out and bring the losses to her heavenly Father, Jean could forgive. From there her relationship with her mother took a major turn. There was nothing to be angry about now; Mom no longer needed to repay her.

Jean realized that her mother never had what she needed in the first place. In Jean's eyes, her mother went from being a powerful inflictor of pain to the needy lost soul who had no comfort for others or herself. In the end, Jean became a safe place for her mother to grieve. Jean led her mother to Christ several years later as the mother lay on her deathbed.

It is not unusual for us to cycle through the stages of grief more than once. This will be determined by the depth of loss and the initial delay before the onset of grief. Normally, we continue cycling through the stages of grief until the issues are completely resolved. Sometimes, we repeat partial cycles of the first three or four stages until we're finally ready to move toward resolution.

Every time we block our grief, we become stuck. The most common way we do this is by demanding of those in our present-day life to meet the unpaid debts of significant others from the past. I see this again and again in my counseling practice with people's attitudes toward authority figures.

Bosses, pastors, politicians, principals, doctors, etc. often take the heat of conflicted people who have never faced the ways their parents have fallen short of giving them what they needed as children.

Generally, there is some present-day element of frustration with the authority figure, which is valid, but by the intensity of the reaction it is clear to see the person is expecting way too much from the person with whom they are angry. None of these people in positions of authority owe you what your parents owed you and no amount of beating on them will produce it!

Expecting others to be responsible for our unresolved grief issues keeps us from God and the truth. It produces destructive behavior. Our symptoms will persist and augment. We may resort to some form of addictive behavior to medicate our pain. Unresolved grief may feed various addictions, extramarital affairs, lack of joy and aliveness, etc.

I was an expert at delayed grief. When we returned from the mission field, I was an emotional and psychological wreck. But I still refused to consider myself as the problem—namely that I needed to grieve. I sought medical help from a psychiatrist. I was relieved to hear that I had a "chemical imbalance" and this was the cause of all my problems.[56]

This supposed that getting my chemicals in order would alleviate my symptoms. A few years and several medications later, I was still depressed and suffering from anxiety. So, I tried special lights. I would sit in front of these full spectrum lights for hours a day. Still, I got no results. Exercise and changing eating patterns didn't change a thing, as well.

During this time an elderly woman approached me and suggested that I may have some unforgiveness towards my mother. I was furious and curtly let the woman know she was wrong. "What a pushy person," I thought. "Just like my mother." From then on, I avoided her and scowled every time she came to mind.

---

[56]I am not discounting a chemical imbalance as a diagnosis but that was not the case with me.

For many years, I thought my parents were faultless. I denied their part in my childhood losses. My unwillingness to face my pain kept me in a state of untruth. Because I refused to be angry with my parents, my anger came out at others. My anger also came out toward myself. I couldn't let myself express this anger. So, I buried it somewhere deep inside. My depression was a by-product of the ever-present but unexpressed anger. It also manifested itself as a deep sadness that I couldn't express. Repressed fear and guilt would show itself as anxiety.

The bargaining that is part of grief can be a place where we get stuck as well. The chronic insistence that others make our lives right is truly magical thinking. The way we keep running from one self-help book or seminar to another implies we really think we are going to fix this mess ourselves.

Other evidence of being stuck in the grief process can be bitterness, resentment, resignation, hopelessness, and the lack of the desire to live. Some characteristics of good grief and impaired grief are listed below:

Healthy Grief	Impaired Grief
1. Shock	1. Denial
2. Anger	2. Chronic Anger
3. Sadness	3. Chronic Depression
4. Bargaining	4. Magical Thinking
5. Forgiveness/and Resolution	5. Unforgiveness/Recycle through the process

Negative emotions, if not tended to, can cause psychosomatic reactions within a person's physical body. If we won't or can't get those emotions out through our feelings, we may find our bodies taking over the role of expressing them. Conditions such as high blood pressure, heart disease, colitis, arthritis, asthma, headaches, and, even cancer can develop from the strain of attempting to hold negative emotions from expression and even awareness. Though these physical problems result from psychological issues, they are still real.

Underlying feelings find expression somehow. Often, they manifest through defense mechanisms that significantly impair or interrupt relationships. As we've already seen, buried anger will eventually be displaced onto something or someone else. Becoming stuck in one of the stages of grief causes depression, usually low-grade, but in some cases serious.

Sometimes people with bulimia or anorexia nervosa are stuck in the bargaining/magical thinking stage. They think that by not allowing themselves to eat, or by purging themselves, they will make their loss less severe, or it will give them self-control over their feelings or over other people. We also sometimes make inner vows: we'll never allow ourselves to need anyone else, we'll never be sexual, we will always rescue others. While we are in pain, our focus is on ourselves. We are, therefore, self-centered or selfish.

The answer isn't to address our symptoms, but to attend to the losses that created them. God wants to take us there far more than we want to go there. He is faithful, and everything He does to orchestrate our healing He does in love to bring us back to communion and harmony with Himself, as well as joyful living. As we will see in Part 2, we recreate the unresolved dramas of our life again and again until either we resolve the issue through grieving, or we finally die.

We want to look further at some of the by-products of impaired grief in our next chapter and how the enemy of our souls tries to keep us captured into a dull, uninspired state of "this is the way it is and there is nothing I can do about it."

Chapter 10—Role of Resignation in Delayed Grief[57]

Delayed grief will cause us to lose zest for life. It will slowly take our energy and leave us without the expectation that things can ever improve. If you observe small children, you see how game they are for life. Babies exude how much they want to live and live to the fullest. They broadcast "I'm here" and expect others to respond to that and delight in them. They are plucky and full of fight!

Grief is the God-given tool for getting rid of hurt, making peace and finally forgiving. This results in plenty of room in our souls for more of God's joie de vivre: peace, adventure, curiosity, hope, enjoyment and pleasure, accomplishment and the list go on and on.

My co-worker, Richard Kinney came upon these insights into resignation through his work with a client. John[58] was a strong believer and often traveled on mission trips with a renowned healer. They witnessed the blind seeing and lame people walking and many other miraculous healings on these trips. Richard had been mentoring John and asked him why he never asked this healer with whom he was very close, to pray for his chronic pain. It was very curious to Richard that requesting help from such an obvious source was not something John had automatically done. It was at that point that Richard began to recognize the role of resignation in the believer's life.

Resignation cons a person into the false assumption that "there is nothing to do to make things change." Or, "my efforts will only result in failure, so why try?" Resignation on the surface looks like a seamless floor that we are so used to, we take it for granted. And beneath it lurk hopeless/despair and other evils that scare us into leaving resignation in place. We reason that resignation is a better choice than feeling

---

[57] My thanks to Richard Kinney for permitting me to expand and illustrate his teaching on resignation.
[58] Not his real name, of course.

hopeless/despair. And it would be except that we can get rid of both through Jesus Christ. Here is an idea for prayer:

"Lord Jesus, I ask that you expose the top seamless surface of resignation in me and tear it up then pump and remove the lies underneath." The floor is hard to see, and many say, "I don't have resignation." But upon further investigation they discover they have quite a lot.

God is a God of answers and solutions. It was Jesus who said, "knock and the door will be opened and seek, and you will find." He is heavily invested in helping us to be cleansed from every negative and destructive reaction. Just look at creation. There's joy, even in the animal kingdom. You can watch puppies play, dolphins swim, birds sing. Birds like singing—they don't have to sing. God could have made the world in grey-tone, not color. And why use more than one color? The extravagance and variety of creation broadcasts the "aliveness" that is the "way it should be."

Most of us are living well below our potential in terms of joy and energy and effectiveness. One of our main roles as counselors is to restore people to their natural levels of effectiveness, joy and success. And as God aids us to excavate this debris in the soul, we always want to fill it with the Father's love, optimism, energy, and good health.

Scattered hopes and dreams are often the reason resignation begins to lay its tiles in our souls. When resignation takes a hold of you, your deepest held belief causes things to which you're resigned, to happen. Such as "People don't like me", "life is hard", "people don't cooperate with me", "I can't make any friends". It's a different song and dance for each different person, but there are many commonalities. "Life's a drudge", some version of "life's a bummer then you die."

Some call this "self-fulfilling prophecy." If we hold lies as truth, now without knowing it, we are praying against ourselves. And as our history becomes more and more filled with these negative life experiences in answer to our hidden prayers, we refer to our "history" as concrete evidence these lies are valid! Do you see how this vicious cycle can keep us stuck in a lackluster life at best and deep discouragement at worst?

When we have not dealt with loss in a timely fashion our hearts can become hard. Some of the various by-products of delayed grief begin to fill our souls. Besides the obvious unforgiveness that accompanies unresolved hurts, there are four other "soul conditions" we want to talk about here. Our Lord wants to help us to make more room for connection with Him and He will help us to address each of these things that contribute to our hard and negatively full hearts. This list is not exhaustive but very helpful.

1. Resentment
2. Bitterness
3. Resignation
4. Hopeless/Despair

Resentment is a feeling of indignant displeasure or persistent ill will at something regarded as a wrong, insult, or injury.[59] Ever find yourself mulling over some situation or relationship where you got hurt and couldn't resolve it? That is the feeling of resentment and as we get older, we can pile up more and more of it! When we reach a certain threshold of resentment and it increasingly becomes a lifestyle, that's where we become full of bitterness.

Bitterness is supported in our soul by a stance that God or whoever was supposed to help us, did not. Our worldview if we become bitter takes on an acrid quality of disappointment and negativity. Rather than hopeful expectation, we anticipate things will not go well for us. No

---

[59] https://www.merriam-webster.com/dictionary/resentment.

wonder the Bible warns of someone who can defile many by a bitter root.[60]

Resignation is where we say: *My difficulty, my pain, my sorrow, whatever I am facing—there is no way I can beat it or get away from it, so I am just going to give up and become resigned to it as a way to lesson my own pain.* As a child, it is true we can't walk away from an abusing or annoying parent. Or as an adult we can't walk away from a medical condition. Resignation is never really a good choice for us because we were created to be aggressive, to be warriors, to be proactive. As adults we can always move back against situations that are unfair even if they are larger than we can face openly. We can always pray against them, invoking God's will and kingdom to enter every circumstance.

But there is an even more compelling purpose to form this false floor of resignation. When we encounter life situations where we have no solution, this provokes in us feelings of hopeless/despair. That negative emotion is one of the most painful feelings we can experience so we are very interested in avoiding it, if possible. When hopeless/despair fills an area of our souls, we can cover it up with resignation and pretend it isn't there. We choose to settle for the dull ache of resigning ourselves to whatever life serves us rather than face the pit of hopeless/despair beneath it.

One of the signs that a person has hopeless/despair is when they must go around things instead of straight at them. They take an overly feminine approach to issues because they are afraid of confronting the hopeless/despair.

The fourplex of resignation, bitterness, resentment and hopeless/despair provide seemingly convincing evidence that you can't go any deeper in life's pursuits.

Deep happiness for you? Nah. A little bit of happiness for you? Yeah, maybe. A life with deep friendships? Nah. Just some casual connections if I

---

[60] See Hebrews 12:15.

get lucky. A lot of success for you? Nah. A little bit of success for you? Maybe.

There is no safety for you in the floor of resignation. Everything beneath it (resentment, bitterness, and hopelessness/despair) are not your friends[61]. It slowly takes your energy and robs your life of joy and pleasure.

My friend and co-worker, Richard Kinney, likes to go after the hopeless/despair in a person first. He treats it like moray eels silently slithering through the person's soul. One of their goals is to make it especially difficult to deal with the other negative qualities inhibiting the person.

The task before us looks insurmountable. The negative threats of resentment, resignation, bitterness and hopeless/despair have thwarted us. But we can start breaking them apart. Imagine that there is a 30-pound block of ice blocking my way and I have a hammer in my hand. Who is going to win? Me or the block of ice? I am going to win. Even if it takes me some time, I am going to pound on that block of ice until it is all little ice chips. That's the situation we are in. Even though this may be a work that takes some time, we can win out against resignation and everything we thought it was protecting us from. With Jesus Christ we are more than conquerors who strengthens us, so we don't have to give up

Even people in prison or those who are being tortured don't have to give up. There are small choices we can make both in prayer and outwardly that make a difference. Richard Wurmbrand was a Romanian Pastor who spent fourteen years in communist prisons suffering for his faith in Christ. When he wasn't in solitary confinement, he endured physical torture and exposure to long periods of hunger and freezing temperatures. In prison, he was given one slice of bread per week for food. Every tenth week, he would "tithe" his food... giving the entire slice to a weaker prisoner as an act of obedience to

---

[61] You may also find plenty of unforgiveness, hatred, jealousy, envy, malice, etc.

64

God.[62] Even by that small of a choice he remained not resigned to his fate even though he couldn't break out of jail or kill his captors.

So, resignation is this floor inside your soul and hidden beneath it are concrete blocks making it very difficult for you to swim and flow with the Spirit of God. Our goal is be increasingly lifted-up in a weightless state able to receive the gentle nudges of the Holy Spirit moving us. If our hearts are heavy and hard, God has to use quite a bit more muscle to get us to turn and go in a different or new direction.

Be suspicious if you always have an explanation as to why "things happen to me like this all the time." You look at your track record and feel you can prove that people in churches don't like you, or that when you start a new program someone's going to disdain it.

This is not at all like little children. Little kids expect to be successful. When they draw a picture and show you, they expect you to clap. They rejoice in whatever they can do and assume others will rejoice with them. They invite us to share their pleasure at accomplishing whatever they do simply because it is their life and they love it!

We, too, can enjoy and appreciate our own personal best. Even if I'm not the best artist, I can have a good day. Most of us are in some way gifted and very lovely given an opportunity. And we give ourselves that opportunity by allowing God to help us remove any resentment, bitterness, resignation and hopeless/despair that has weighed down our souls. I pray for you right now that the energy and love of God would begin to pull up out of you any and all this debris as you open your heart and expectations to Him.

All that we are speaking of here is part of what it takes to deal with the effects of delayed grief. The idea that we need to settle for all this soft coal packed down in our souls repressing and suffocating our real potential is based on lies. *"That's just the way I feel, that always happens*

---

[62] Quoted from Troy Gramling website: https://troygramling.com/giving-bread/

65

to me.” Whatever your story is, we have got to realize that the son or daughter of God has possibilities that we don't often see expressed around us.

If we seek God to show us whatever walls of unbelief have constrained us to live much smaller than we were meant to live, He will reveal to us the foundational lies that keep those walls in place. Here are just a few of those lies:

I don't belong.
I will never really be loved.
I am a disappointment to others, and they will eventually disappoint me.
I should never have been born.
The world is a hostile place. People are always out to hurt me.

“Everything is dumbed down in most Christian venues to the point where we look pretty good when we are really not doing that well. If we can rise above this the Lord will propel us into something that looks more like Jesus Christ being manifest on the earth. I think we would see more miracles, genuine joy and salvations based on people saying *I want what that guy has. Whatever he has, I don't know what that is, but I want that.* I don't think many Christians are witnesses like that, but I think they could be.”[63]

Richard and I have helped many clients with resignation problems as described above and seen very good fruit. Ridding yourself of resignation and lies will make it easier for you to connect to the spirit man.

The key to becoming fully alive is in our spirit man (gender non-specific) who is already inside of us. The grieving process God placed within us will guide us out of misery. Our spirit man can lead us into a vibrant and joyful life.

---

[63] From a conversation I recorded with Richard Kinney, my co-worker at Firehouse Ministries, Inc.

Most Christians are unaware of their spirit man. But this powerful part of us can mentor and coach each area of our souls into communion and harmony with Jesus Christ. Our spirit man and how he can help us is the subject of our next chapter.

Chapter 11—Role of the Spirit Man in Grieving

We don't want to only talk about a happy and productive life. We want to wake up each day being excited about being who we are and what we have. The great big wonderful God of the entire universe is interested in you even when you are not doing anything important. He invites us to be invaded by His kingdom. He calls us to a resurrected life—the breathing in of heaven—which follows an exhaling of all the heaviness and corruption that believing lies has dumped upon us. The part of us which ushers in such a resurrected life is our spirit man.

All that I have been telling you in this book about grieving and emptying out the negative residue that contaminates your soul is meant to bring your spirit man into prominence in you. As we live more and more out of our spirit man, he becomes the mentor, encourager and power source for our soul and body. How? Because he is already connected to God and full of the power and love of the Holy Spirit. The spirit man develops the mind, will and emotions towards alignment with the life of Christ and the flow of the Holy Spirit to the point where our spirits glow with His infusion.

One day I was working with a woman and had a vision of her soul. The spirit part of her looked like a pipeline from heaven wanting to flow living waters into her mind, will and emotions, but the end of the pipe where it met her soul was blocked with different colors of cement. The cement represented unresolved grief, resentment, unforgiveness, bitterness, resignation, etc.

The spirit man (gender non-specific) is the part of us that is a molecule of God and that sits in the heavenly places in Christ *right now*. It is our inner sanctuary and has the means to bring the transformational power of the Holy Spirit to our thinking, our feelings, our wills and our bodies. As we grieve our losses, we are facing what is in our souls and allowing the love of God via our spirit man to invade that area and align it with God's way of seeing us. We also receive His touch and His presence, so we are no longer alone and without help and comfort.

68

Paul talks about the spirit man but very few people know that you can connect to that wonderful part of yourself. Try the following exercise alone.

Pray that God the Father and Jesus will help you connect to this best part of you—your spirit man. While your soul, your mind, your will and your body all need discipline and boundaries, this part of you, your spirit man, just needs to be experienced. Take time every day to practice experiencing your deepest, most powerful self. Allowing your thinking or emotions to occupy all your attention is counterproductive to Spirit-filled living.

Dedicating ourselves to acknowledge and connect to our spirit man provides an internal energy and guidance system. Then the mind, will, emotions and body will be infused with the Godly energy and clarity that just being near this best part of you imparts. Like a hot blazing log burns and causes a cold log to catch on fire, the spirit man sets the rest of the soul ablaze with the fire and warmth it carries from God.

The portal for the unconditional love to invade the soul is the spirit man. Imagine you are a dolphin and you deep dive into the ocean. You effortlessly swim towards a shimmering ball of radiant energy where you can enter and find rest and peace and comfort. That is a great picture of what we are doing as we go deep within ourselves and concentrate on the part of ourselves that is already connected to heaven and bonded to God.

We all need both the help of God and the help of people to be transformed. I received many hours of help from individuals who listened to me and tried to help me grieve. They constantly referred me to my relationship with God in Christ to help this process. I needed their intervention to begin since I had such a muddled picture of God based on my faulty assumption that He was like my parents.

Since then, I have a regular practice of recognizing and connecting to the Lord through my spirit man. I sit silently in God's presence and receive whatever "daily bread" He has for me. Sometimes it leads me to healing and restores my soul, other times it is simply the joy of encountering the wonder that is Him. During my regular time with Him, He is feeding me His manna for that day.

I believe that both safe human and divine environments are important for good grief to take place. I wish every church could be a supportive family structure that offers people such an opportunity for sanctuary. But ultimately God gives us what we need, and people, however wonderful, will never be perfect. The best scenario we can hope for is a combination of the two. Trustworthy people help us to grow in trusting God. Knowing God is faithful will make it easier for us to have faith in people by recognizing the ones He has put in our lives to love on us. Being full of God gives us an overflow of love for those around us even when they don't have much to offer.

God is after a deep and powerful transformation in our souls. Imagine your soul as His personal Garden which He lovingly cares for and husbands. He will cheerfully pull up weeds, turn over soil, add fertilize and nurture both beautiful and fruitful plants particular to you, His unique creation. As the Holy Spirit rearranges and prunes us, He is quite cheerful about things dying in the garden that are hindering the joy, peace, love and goodness He knows belongs there. This process of dying to the old and becoming alive to the new plays out in nature all around us. Our transformation follows this pattern as well.

We are promised that if we are united with Christ in His death then we will also share in His resurrection. The resurrection He invites us to, is a here and now event as well as a ticket to heaven. Our heavenly inheritance is meant to be accessed in our lives now—not only in our afterlife!

To further advanced on our path of being led by our spirit man full of the Holy Spirit, we will need to repent of whatever God shows us that has been out of alignment with His ways and to be delivered from the footholds of the enemy that we have cooperated with. These two concepts, repentance and deliverance which pave the way for us in revealing the spirit man within are the subjects of our next chapter.

Chapter 12—Role of Deliverance and Repentance in Transformation

Paul speaks of the footholds of the enemy concerning unresolved anger in Ephesians 4:27. Any negative emotions we harbor are areas of our souls where demons can manipulate and torment us. We may imagine demons to be horned red beings who only manifest through frothing mouths and loud screams. We rarely detect their presence in our thinking. They can present themselves as accusations of ourselves and others. Or as any other tormenting thoughts of unhappy events or emotions needling us. More often than not, if they are there, then it is mostly because we are cooperating with their beliefs.

Deliverance from the footholds of the enemies is needed once a believer is ready to turn away from the false beliefs in their souls and to let go of the negative emotions around those lies. When I lead a person in repentance, part of it is for them to renounce all cooperation with the enemy and his lies. Any believer who is willing to turn from evil, is already taking away the reason why the demons can stay.

As we live more and more out of our spirit man, the inconsistencies and twisting in our souls will be highlighted and we will no longer want to act out of those false beliefs. Our spirit man is like a loving and discipling father figure inside of us meant to coach, inspire and lovingly correct all our thinking and wills, and to affirm, contain and direct our emotions.

Experiencing God's unconditional love opens the door for us to be capable of loving others sincerely. Once we get happy about being who we are, the beloved and cherished child of the most important Person in the universe, we begin to live in a bubble of positivity about our life and our possibilities. This flows into our perception and treatment of others. It is impossible to love others without first loving ourselves.

Once we recognize and accept how cherished and accepted, we are by our Father, God, we will stop demanding others to make our lives right and instead desire to share with them the riches of His love in our hearts.

Dying to our losses awakens us to God's provision. As we allow the flood of His devotion to us to overtake every other belief system, we will want to turn from[64] our need to control or manipulate, our devotion to the accumulation of wealth and things, our craving for recognition and praise, our selfish insistence on being right and having the last word, our habit of always putting our comfort and well-being above that of others, our own empire building, just to name a few!

From the safety of His love we will be amazed at our ability to face unsavory issues in our souls. We will progress, as Paul did, to seeing ourselves as a chief of sinners who has experienced unexplainable and immeasurable grace and lives in great joy because of it. It will become easier to feel compassion and to extend grace to others in their failings, having experienced deeply the patience and perseverance of God towards us in our many faults. Truly the one who has been forgiven much loves much![65] We become like Him in loving mercy.

Our repentance follows the same process of grieving detailed above. For example, pride is any attitude that puts us as the center of the universe. This can be done in a positive way of seeing oneself as superior and entitled. Or it can be done in a negative way of seeing oneself as the horrible person who just can't be good enough, do enough or keep everyone else happy. This pattern can sometimes be mistaken as "humility." Here is a step by step description of someone grieving or repenting of pride in their soul:

- We come out of denial about how proud we are.
- We may feel indignant and angry at first that God would show us this about ourselves or we may be furious at "how bad we are".

---

[64] The true meaning of the word repentance is "to turn away from."
[65] Luke 7:47.

- Next, we will feel sad that we aren't any better than the last person we may have judged for being proud. We had expected more from ourselves!
- In depression, we will begin to face our own powerlessness and how without His transformational power at work within us, we will never change.
- We may then try to bargain a little, questioning if this really is as bad as it looks or if we must let it go. Or we may imagine we are powerful enough to change ourselves. Here we decide to give in to God's way of seeing our pride and dealing with it.
- Finally, we must fully accept the responsibility for our pride. We confess it and face the consequences flowing from it. We become willing to do things differently, to see things in a new light.
- Here we accept God's forgiveness and are reconciled to Him. Our repentance will be heartfelt. It won't be a superficial head exercise.
- We will then notice a CHANGE in our lives. For those with a superiority complex, they become more honoring of others and willing to allow them to shine. For those who held themselves as a negative center of the universe, they show a new level of kindness and acceptance of their humanity.

It is always a temptation to blame others or even God for our own sin. Considering where we need to change is the first big step. Rather than obsessing about our "badness" we can be thankful the Holy Spirit is pointing out areas in our lives where things are not going well with our soul. And it is only by God's mercy that we can ever dare to admit the sin in our hearts. It is by God's kindness that we are led to repentance.[66]

Grieving our losses will move our Christianity out of our heads and out of the pews and into the inner being of our hearts as well as the lives of our children, spouses, extended families, co-workers, neighbors and friends. It will allow us to see ourselves and others as we truly are:

---

[66] Romans 2:4. Repentance is not feeling badly about ourselves, it is a decision to turn and go in another way.

- Children of a loving God with amazing potential.
- A person who gives God joy simply by belonging to Him.
- Broken people full of wounding at the hands of sin.
- Characters whose resentment and bitterness can poison all those around them.[67].
- People separated from their loving Creator who crave without knowing it what only He can provide.

Have we accepted a mandate of "Doing is more important than being?" Some church leaders will cruelly shout from the pulpit to their wounded flocks, "Get over your problems and serve God!" The implication is that if we start acting like we're healed, we'll be healed! This is unfortunately not true. It is manipulation by guilt at worst and serious denial at best. They dress the wound of my people as though it were not serious. "Peace, peace" they say, when there is no peace.[68]

Could this be the reason many missionaries and pastors fall like wounded soldiers in heated battle? They give their all and when they are used up, the church banishes them in shame and disgrace. Often the sickest people in the church are the most active. They are desperately seeking Daddy's approval. Even though they give their bodies, so to speak, to be burned, they have not love.[69] God's love is something they keep hoping to be able to give to others but have never received for themselves.

Deliverance and repentance are an important part of the sanctifying work of the Holy Spirit. Time and energy must be devoted to such activities as well as the grieving process. Otherwise we will be shallow, broken and empty. To pour out kindness and care to those around us, we need to have first experienced it for ourselves. How can we have something to give when we have not received well? If we are already full of such things as unresolved loss, resentment, bitterness, etc. there will be little room for all the good we

---

[67] Romans 3:16-17. "Ruin and misery mark their ways and the way of peace they do not know"
[68] Jeremiah 6:14.
[69] 1 Corinthians 13:3.

hope to offer to others—not to mention our desire to be happy and satisfied in our own lives.

We don't want to add the church to the list of places where we give but don't receive. It just makes more demands on an already demanding life. You don't heal a broken arm by exercising it. It must be realigned and then protected from stress and strain. Once mended, it can slowly be used again and then move into vigorous retraining and exercise. You may be thinking, "This grieving process is too time-consuming. Surely God could not be orchestrating it."

Jesus spent thirty years being prepared for ministry, communing with the Father and being part of a family. Moses had a forty-year internship that began when he was already 40 years old. Paul took eleven years of hidden growth before he began his ministry in earnest. Abraham was still having conflicts and learning from them in his eighties.

David was called a man after God's own heart. Did he have many conflicts with his family? His own father forgot to mention him as one of his sons when the renowned prophet visited his home. His brothers despised him and didn't see him as very important. In the Psalms David says things like, "Even though your father and mother forsake you, I will receive you.[70]" And "You knit me together in my mother's womb."[71]

Now why do you think he said those kinds of things? He had wounding there, places where his soul needed to be restored. David married Saul's daughter, Michal, who then treated him with the same scorn as his parents and brothers. Did David pass on to his children his unresolved grief, treating them with the same aloofness and disconnect with which he had been reared? It appears he did.

Did David seek to pacify his profound loneliness and isolation with an affair? Yes. David never resolved all his conflicts, but the psalms paint a

---

[70] Psalm 27:10.
[71] See Psalm 139.

record of his constant grieving: his facing his losses, his anger and sadness, his depression and bargaining and finally, at the end of almost every psalm his encounters with God. Such was the life of a man who was deemed, "after God's own heart.[72]"

Are we above these great people of faith? Are we going to be a fast and instant spirituality that defies the years necessary for maturation and depth? I don't think so. We can just continue in our proud denial at the cost of living spiritually shallow lives that look like massive leafy trees, but which never produce any good fruit.

> "But the fruit of the Spirit is love, joy, peace, patience, kindness,
> goodness, faithfulness, gentleness and self-control.
> Against such things there is no law."[73]

And as well:

> "If I speak in the tongues of men and of angels, but have not love,
> I am only a resounding gong or a clanging cymbal.
> If I have the gift of prophecy and can fathom all mysteries
> and all knowledge, and if I have a faith that can move mountains,
> but have not love, I am nothing.
> If I give all I possess to the poor and surrender my body to the flames,
> but have not love, I gain nothing."[74]

Spiritual gifts, knowledge, faith, service, and sacrifice are all things that we do. They flow out of who we are. Who we are is intimately related to our losses and the losses we have inflicted? If we don't know God's love in these basic places of our souls, then we are lacking. What we do will not change who we are, only the communion of relationship both with God and others in our most vulnerable parts will transform us into the image of Christ.

---

[72] Acts 13:22—Paul quoting 1Samuel 13:14.
[73] See Galatians 5:22.
[74] 1 Corinthians 13:1-3.

Jesus leads us in the process of grief. By making Himself available to us by His Presence and by having paved the way of dealing with His own losses before us, He will be the One carrying us along in this painful but fruitful process. He is bringing us to joy, that is the goal as well as Oneness with Him.

Now that we have investigated in detail grief, we need to look more closely at the ways unresolved grief issues show themselves in our daily lives. In part two, our goal is to identify and resolve the past in a way that it no longer gets repeated. We will use many examples from people's lives to demonstrate these patterns and how to trace backwards to the roots of losses that created them.

Part 2—Identify and Resolve Your Past

Chapter 13—Life Patterns Emerge

Sometimes we are completely unaware of the reasons behind the patterns in our lives. If we keep repeating certain themes in our life situations, we could be pursuing hidden and destructive agendas. It takes wisdom and understanding to discern the reasons and purpose of our agenda. We formulate these secret agendas based on a series of losses from earlier in life. Without knowing it, we are demanding of the people in our present-day life to pay debts from long ago that a significant other never paid. An insistence that we will get from others all that we feel they owe us is a way of trying to save our own lives.

> For whoever wants to save their life will lose it,
> but whoever loses their life for me will find it.[75]

We internalize the trauma of our younger years, adopt it as "the way it's supposed to be", and create our worldview around it. Unfortunately, no matter how crazy or unfortunate our life, it becomes a model of what we consider "normal." From there, without realizing it, we draw people and situations to us that are like our family. We have present day conflicts where we are trying subconsciously to repeat our early drama. We believe this time we will make it work. The reason we are unlikely to succeed, is that our real need is for transformation, not cooperation from outside sources to redo and complete our early dramas. Plus, those we choose to help us "work it out" generally have similar issues as our family! Great theory but it doesn't work.

> A plan in the heart of a man is like deep water,
> But a man of understanding draws it out.[76]

---

[75] Matthew 16:25, NIV.

[76] Proverbs 20:5

Below I have created a hypothetical person, Rebecca, to illustrate these points.

Rebecca stared at the phone in her hand. The person at the other end had hung up abruptly. Rebecca wondered how a good friend could treat her so rudely. She had recently began attending a support group for divorcees and made a couple friends. After a few months, it looked like the honeymoon in these relationships was over. The small group of women had turned on her like so many other former friends. Rebecca had no explanation for it.

She turned her thoughts to work. Her supervisor at the warehouse was harassing her again, asking the impossible, she felt. After she left her last position, she believed this would take care of her problems. No such luck!

For a moment, Rebecca scanned the panorama of her life. Unhappy home life as a child, years of studying to be a social worker only to quit at her first position rather than be fired; a marriage ended in divorce, several churches joined and abandoned. The list of hopeful contacts and the ensuing ruined relationships were too painful to ponder for more than a few moments.

In her view, people were so mean and rejecting. Why weren't people kinder to her? Then, a daunting thought passed through her mind. What if it was something she was doing? Was that possible?

Does history seem to painfully repeat itself in your life, like in Rebecca's? Do you ever wonder why you feel stuck in certain unhealthy relationship patterns? Or wonder why things always seem to turn out disappointingly the same? Like a hamster on a wheel, you keep running along the same path and can't get off?

Are there certain "trigger" situations in your life in which someone says or does something that pushes a button inside of you and sets in motion negative reactions, feelings and behaviors? Do you get out of one crazy-making relationship just to fall into another?

The Scripture says that we reap what we sow. One application of this concept carries over into our perceptions and how we react to situations and people. It would imply that we carry a hidden set of perceptions into every relationship, into every situation. We sow those expectations and reap a harvest which looks very much like our earliest relational connections.

For over 25 years, I have worked with people and seen plenty of confirming evidence for the presence of destructive patterns in their lives. Helping them decipher these patterns and grieve the early losses connected to them leads to new possibilities for change in both their way of seeing themselves and others.

The first step is admitting their part in the drama. Next, they need to stop seeing themselves or anyone else as being enough to "make this right". They will need to find in their relationship with Jesus Christ the love, value, worth and acceptance that will finally satisfy their deepest longings.

This is not an instantaneous process but a series of relational interchanges with God and loving people to begin to build new relational bridges within. And all the destruction from the painful, broken bridges must be repaired over time.

The degree of healing in their lives depends on three things:

1. Accepting the reality of the losses that creates their reactions
2. Grieving their losses
3. Coming to know God's provision instead

Before they received healing, they were bound to their losses. They needed a key to unlock them from their losses and repeating the destructive patterns over and over. Our goal is to be freed from our past and instead, be connected to the present moment in a joyful, productive and effective way.

Rebecca's life demonstrated this sorry pattern of replaying her losses many times. Was it just coincidence that her relationships followed a similar course whether at home, work, or social life? Could it be that she carried inside a way of viewing herself, her world, and her friends? As her life unfolded, she was interpreting each event and reaction through a filter in her heart. Her vision affected her reactions because she saw circumstances based on experiences in her past.

One of the writers who helped me deepen my insights into the dilemma of destructive and repetitive life patterns was an internationally known psychoanalyst, Alice Miller. She had practiced psychoanalysis for over twenty years only to resign when she discovered that addressing the traumatic losses of childhood could heal patients rather than symbol-laden psychoanalysis. In the *Afterward to the Second Edition* of her book *For Your Own Good*, she says:

For some years now, it has been possible to prove, through new therapeutic methods, that repressed traumatic experiences of childhood are stored up in the body and, though unconscious, exert an influence even in adulthood. In addition, electronic testing of the fetus has revealed a fact previously unknown to most adults—that a child responds to and learns both tenderness and cruelty from the very beginning.

In the light of this new knowledge, even the most absurd behavior reveals its formerly hidden logic once the traumatic experiences of childhood need no longer remain shrouded in darkness.

Whereas these studies focused on the more traumatic occurrences in childhood, again and again I saw in my practice that even small losses strung over the years of childhood were leaving their imprint on people's lives. Even people with "good" parents were reacting to losses of some kind or another.

What then is the solution? How do you help people get over their losses that may date back as far as the womb itself? Everyone needs to have God give them what was denied. Each person is created by God with His love set as a default. Anything less creates losses more serious than we ever let ourselves admit.

82

Let me explain. God crafted our inmost being with the idea that we would have a twenty-four hour a day, seven days a week relationship with Him. He designed our hearts to receive His unconditional and unfailing love. He meant for the people surrounding us to be unbroken vessels of His love. That is what leaves us so vulnerable, sensitive and open as infants. There is no protection against evil because it was not part of the original plan for our environment.

But, of course, we aren't born into Eden. Instead we appear in a womb of a human who has fallen short of the glory and purposes of God. From then on, our relationships may be well-intended but still fall short of what we were created for.

The losses in Rebecca's life began early on. She had been the youngest of several siblings. She was never close or well-liked by any of her siblings. Her mother would give in to her demands but at the same time scorn her and berate her as inferior.

Rebecca's siblings resented how her neediness dominated the family system. They tolerated Rebecca's presence but did not enjoy a relationship with her. This resulted in Rebecca behaving as a bully, insisting on having her own way, but perceiving herself as a victim who was being bullied by others.

Rebecca was reaping perceptions and wounding that had been sown early on. Rebecca became a professing Christian in college and expected that all should be different in her life now. She knew she would go to heaven when she died. But life in the meantime hadn't changed dramatically—as she had hoped. Rebecca was suffering from "unresolved grief issues".

Let me briefly summarize our discussion from Part 1. Unresolved grief is produced by any type of loss in a person's life which has never been properly expressed and resolved.

When we speak of losses, most people think of major life events such as a death in the family, bankruptcy or other traumatic happenings. Yet there are many losses, small losses, which plague our days here on earth. Because we are created to receive perfect love from a perfect Heavenly Father, our journey here on earth where we are separated from that perfect love is riddled with pain and loss. The imperfect human love our parents give us creates many losses from the time we appear in our mother's womb. Added to those losses are our own bad choices which have a destructive result.

David, the Psalmist, was aware of the need for laying hold of God's presence in the womb. Ps. 139 declares God's presence with him there. I do not believe this was poetry. I think it was a transformational experience for David to encounter the truth of God's love for him and presence with him all the way back to his conception. David was practicing the presence of God for his past. Psalm 22 has a more poignant and painful rendition of this need.

> Yet you brought me out of the womb;
> You made me trust in you even at my mother's breast.
> From birth I was cast upon you;
> From my mother's womb, you have been my God.[77]

Psalm 22 is also a Messianic Psalm that pertains to the life of Christ. He took on human flesh and all its limitations, but He demonstrated for us all dependency on the Heavenly Father to remedy all the losses and suffering of earth.

Such an encounter with God is what we all need to repair life's revolving door of conflicts and relational problems. An application of the presence of God not just for each present moment, but wherever the past bombards the present with perceptions and attitudes that were formed apart from God's presence, this is what is needed to transform and heal life and to equip us to love with God's love.[78]

---

[77] Psalm 22:9, 10
[78] Everyone also needs new human relationships, as well, to grow in being able to give and receive love.

84

The subject of these perceptions and attitudes and their effect on our lives is the subject of the next chapter.

Chapter 15—Our Perceptions, Our Reactions and Our Responses.

So, what are the components of these unresolved grief issues? Unresolved grief is one of the characteristics of what the Bible calls "the flesh" (see Romans 6-8). For it to die, we must first acknowledge it before we can let it go. Our unresolved grief is comprised of three elements: our perceptions, our reactions and our responses.

- Our *Perceptions*: How we see people, events, circumstances.
- Our *Reactions*: How we think and feel about people, events, circumstances.
- Our *Responses*: How we behave or decisions we make regarding people, events, circumstances.

In other words, why do we see things the way we do (our *perceptions*)? What makes us feel a certain way towards people (our *reactions*)? And why do we then behave the way we do (our *responses)*?

These three components all go back to the underlying belief system within us. Our belief system is that hidden set of rules that we have accepted as true. It is our world view. It is based on the presuppositions from which we make all our interpretations of people, things, and events. Our belief system is our own customized, personalized definition of reality.

Parts of our belief system are known to us, like trusting Jesus as Savior. But other parts are unknown. You may secretly be afraid of people. You may feel unloved and unwanted but have never put that into words. We may be acting on many beliefs which are largely hidden from our awareness.

When our belief system is hidden from our conscious awareness, we will find ourselves repeating certain situations and reactions to those situations over time. At first, we will assume that a force outside of us is causing the problem. But usually by the time we have lived thirty or forty years, we begin to suspect that something is wrong inside of us!

For example, Dave is 45 years old. He has been fired from four jobs over the past fifteen years. He begins each job with a good relationship with his boss and then, when he gets comfortable in his position something always seems to go wrong and he gets fired. Thus, he gets very angry and feels betrayed. The hurt he experiences are so deep that it affects the way he feels about himself as a person. Dave finally, reluctantly agreed to get some help For the first time, Dave is considering that the unresolved grief issues of his life may be responsible for the unhappy drama that seems to repeat itself. He is finally beginning to look at his belief system and how that was formed and how it is affecting his life.

Dave was the oldest son in a family where the father was an alcoholic Dave's father was abusive to his mother and the children for many years Dave believed he had to compensate for his father's shortcomings. He took great initiative for his family and took on tasks well beyond his years. He excelled at most everything he did. Then, when Dave reached puberty, he began to stand up to dad and tried to defend his mother and younger siblings At this point, Dave came into severe conflict with his father who threw him out of the house. Dave then went to live with an aunt where he finished high school and continued with his life. Since then his father has become a Christian and stopped drinking. Their relationship is better than it ever has been.

As Dave shared this information with me, he began to see how his job situations had closely paralleled his home life. He'd start out fine at each job with great expectations. Then in time he would notice faults in his company. He would feel betrayed that they were not meeting his high expectations and believe that it was up to him to do something about it. He'd show great initiative and take on tasks well beyond his responsibilities. He'd even openly confront his employer.

As he linked his present feelings to the past hurt from his relationship with his father, Dave began to weep over the way he had felt betrayed by his dad He felt angry at the abuse and how unjustly his father treated them as a family. He felt the powerlessness of not being able to stop his own pain as well as his mother's and sibling's.

In admitting these feelings, Dave also saw more things about his own belief system. He saw that he felt ashamed of himself as a person. He didn't feel worthwhile unless he was achieving something important. But even then, he still didn't ever feel that what he was doing was important enough. He saw how at work he would threaten his boss by venturing out on his own in his pursuit for significance. This, combined with the mountain of anger he had pent-up against his father, caused him to come off as very aggressive in his endeavors. He finally realized how much he had been contributing to his own dismissals.

I had to help Dave sort through his love/hate relationship with his father. He hated him because he had loved him and hoped for so many good things that never came to pass. Dave addressed his belief system by speaking to his memory of his father like this:

"Dad, I really loved you even though you were mean. Sometimes you were nice to me. I remember you took me fishing and to some ball games. I have been carrying around some hurt and anger toward you that I didn't realize. It's been messing me up at work, so I want to deal with it and forgive you for how you hurt me."

"I am angry at you for throwing me out of the house. I was doing the right thing to stand up to you and try to protect Mom. In fact, all the while growing up, I was trying to do the right thing to try and win your love. I got good grades in school. I tried hard in sports that you liked; I kept my room clean. Now I see how much of what I did was just to try to please you. But in the end, you rejected me when you kicked me out of the family."

Somewhere in this monologue, Dave starts to cry and his face gets red. Grief sweeps over him and he doubles over with the terrible realization that his initiative and extraordinary efforts as a child were not only an attempt to make up for what his father lacked, but also an attempt to win his dad's affection and approval. These attempts were, in the end, in vain. His hidden

88

belief system has plagued him his entire life, and now for the first time, it is being exposed. So much is making sense from his life. He's finally starting to understand the reason for the pattern in the years of hard work and advancement at different jobs only to end by being booted out the door for the same initiative and drive that caused him to rise in the first place!

Let's trace Dave's path to his unresolved grief issues.

- His *perception* was that he was not loved or cherished.
- His *reaction* to this perception was feelings of rejection, shame and anger.
- His *response* to this perception was that he could somehow earn his father's (or that of any authority figure's) love by performance.

Dave is dazed by how much he has contributed to the way his life has progressed. He sees how angry he has been. He has been in a double bind. He was trying to win the love of those most important to him by his own performance. Yet, in the end, his hard-driving performance-related behaviors drove a wedge between himself and those whose love and respect he desired. The separation from them would cause him to become furious with them that he should ever be in the position to have to earn their favor. On the job, he would channel this anger into ambitious projects, but sooner or later the anger would be directed toward his bosses. All along he found them to be lacking in some way and had then despised them for their weaknesses. Now he was seeing them, as well as himself, in a different light.

Dave spoke again to the memory of his dad: "Dad, I wanted your approval with all my heart. But I see now that you just can't give me what I need. I can no longer demand from my bosses to give me that approval. I can't win their approval and then when they don't seem to give it like I want it, I start to find fault with them because they remind me of you, Dad. You failed me. But I'm going to cancel the debt you owe me, Dad, because you can never pay it."

At this point, Dave is ready to move away from the sick attachment to his dad and his expectations that have created a life of unresolved grief. His facing the true root of his anger and feeling the sadness and depression of his loss move him towards letting go of what he never got and never will get out of this relationship. He will use the ongoing relationship he has with the Heavenly Father to take the place of everything he wanted and needed from his earthly father. He can thus begin to taste the relationship that was originally meant to happen, before sin:

"Please forgive me, Father, for trying to protect myself with anger. I have hated my father for what he couldn't give me. I have hated men who reminded me of my father. I accept your role as Father and Creator in my life. You created me. You wanted me. You approve of me apart from my performance. You died to pay for my sins while I was still a sinner. You have proven your commitment to me. I see now my dad couldn't give me the perfect love that only You give. I cancel my dad's debt to me. It's not that he wouldn't give it to me. I see now he didn't have it to give. So, I forgive my dad, Lord. And I confess that I have beaten people up with my anger, just like he did to me. I turn from judging him for what I myself have done to others."

Some of this prayer came up automatically from Dave's heart, other parts I coached him as I felt led by the Spirit. But he meant every word of it from his heart. Dave also renounced all the expectations he had put on his bosses and repented of the anger he had dumped on them that was really meant for his father. The sun had gone down on his anger (Ephesians 4:26-27) and Satan had been able to use it to stir up negative reactions in Dave's lifestyle which caused negative consequences in his life.

Such insight broke down an important barrier in Dave. Over time he would then have to break up all the habits of anger and judgment that had formed from these lies. He would need to replace them with the truth of God that is ministered in our lives by the Holy Spirit.

Each believer has the constant companionship and help of the Holy Spirit. I encourage them to appropriate this help daily through prayer and practicing the presence of God. Learning to feel Him and hear His voice encouraging us and guiding us can repair our broken inner pieces and lead us in a joyful life full of peace with quick recovery from any future losses. A helpful exercise for connecting to God's perception of us is at firehouseministries.com in the free courses called the "Love and Approval of God" by Richard Kinney.

The Holy Spirit, as our Counselor, will help us in identifying our thinking and our feelings that are provoked by our unresolved losses. In the next chapter I hope to open your eyes to see how your interpretation of life and reality may be greatly twisted by what you came to believe was "normal" early on in life.

Chapter 14—How We Interpret Life Changes Everything

One way to illustrate unresolved grief is to interview several different people about how they interpret the same situation. I had the opportunity to do this for several years while I worked for an organization where I ministered to numerous volunteers. Sometimes, I heard about the same problematic situation from several different people. I often knew about their childhoods from my mentoring relationship with them. It was easy to see their "unresolved grief" play itself out in their perception of the problem and how they reacted to other's actions and words.

For illustration purposes, I have created a hypothetical situation where our friend Marcy is in a support group for young mothers and she asks for prayer because she has felt very tired and discouraged lately and not much like being with anyone. There are five other women in the group. To demonstrate my point, let's project what some of the possible perspectives might be to Marcy's request for prayer:

Marcy says, "I need prayer. I have been very discouraged. I just feel like staying home alone and not talking to anyone. Getting to this meeting was a real effort!"

And pretending we can hear their thoughts, here are five plausible responses from the five different perspectives of the women in the prayer meeting:

Juanita: "Poor Marcy! She probably has been doing too much with her family and at church. I'll make sure not to bother calling until she feels better. I wonder if I have been calling her too often?"

Mary: "That Marcy is always feeling sorry for herself. Poor me! Poor me! Why doesn't she grow up? That makes me so mad."

Rose: "Wow! Marcy always looks so together. I didn't think she had any problems! That must be embarrassing to share like that! I'll try to act like I didn't notice."

Sharita: "I wonder if she feels that way because of the argument we had last week about the kids making too much noise during the service. She probably feels like I don't like her anymore."

Tiffany: "I'll stop by and see Marcy tomorrow. Sounds like she needs someone to talk to. That's a terrible way to feel."

Why does each woman react to Marcy in such a different way? The answer lies in a perception filter that each woman carries inside. These filters were created by experiences in their pasts, some of which were negative and created losses in their lives. Without even thinking about it they are following their own rules of relationships. From there they react to Marcy with what each believes is an accurate response to the situation. We can analyze each response and guess what losses, if any, may have produced such reactions to Marcy:

Juanita will ignore Marcy assuming when people are overwhelmed, they prefer to be left alone. Something in her background taught her that going off alone to lick your wounds is safer than making yourself vulnerable to others while in need.

Mary will scorn Marcy, demonstrating her own rule that to be weak and needy is shameful. Somewhere she has probably been treated with disdain when showing her own weakness. This reaction reflects the way she treats herself in such a circumstance.

Rose projects her own need to hide behind a "happy face" onto Marcy. Maybe Rose was taught to keep her chin up and pretend nothing was wrong as a way of coping with loss. Such a fake and unauthentic posture is a great loss itself.

Sharita will try to fix Marcy by taking the blame on herself for Marcy's problem. Her reaction demonstrates some loss that encouraged her to blame herself in trouble. She can control her universe by always being responsible for everyone's feelings.

Tiffany tries to console Marcy in the way she has been comforted many times by those close to her, probably beginning with her mother. She, like the others, offers that which she has received. In her case, it is positive, based on positive rather than negative experiences.

Each of these women has a history of experiences that have formed their belief systems. Out of that belief system they evaluate what Marcy has communicated and then react to their perception of what they believe she is trying to say and, then, act upon it. Each woman's response can be traced to past experiences. If each woman was willing to address their root conflicts, it would be possible for them to change their way of thinking, and, therefore, their reaction to Marcy.

This is just a small slice of each women's life so we can examine it. Sometimes we will have a healthy response to people, other times we will respond out of our unresolved grief and hurt them with the same loss inflicted on us. Once we encounter the love and compassion of God in an experiential way, we will have much more bandwidth for offering that to others.

> Praise be to the God and Father of our Lord Jesus Christ,
> the Father of compassion and the God of all comfort,
> who comforts us in all our troubles,
> so that we can comfort those in any trouble
> with the comfort we ourselves have received from God.[79]

As Christians, the goal for responding to people is to respond as a representative of God and His love for that person. The above verse tells us that this happens when we receive from God and then, in turn, we offer what

---

[79] 2 Corinthians 1:3-4

we have received from Him to them. To see them through His eyes and not our own perceptions is what we want. But our own experiential filter, full of unresolved grief, clouds our vision. Others receive what we have received. And if that is negative and still deeply rooted in us then our earthly heritage will be passed on to others rather than our heavenly heritage which is the unconditional, kind love of God. The Bible talks about the church as being a family—the family of God. Being part of a group of believers who show us God's love is certainly needed and I pray you will be able to benefit from that. Too often, though, there is plenty of talk and very little practice of love.

Above, I have broken down into slow motion a process that takes place continuously and simultaneously. Before long the webs of perceptions, reactions and responses get so thick and entwined that it is very difficult to follow what is happening. It is difficult to define objectively what is happening! It is obvious why our relationships can become strained so quickly at home, church and work.

Other recent studies of the brain have confirmed these phenomena. Due to technology which enables scientists to view and follow brain patterns in living subjects, we now see that emotional responses are embedded in a non-thinking area of the brain[80] which can be triggered by the slightest reminder of a past event or relationship.

As an adult, I experienced this triggering of emotions at a professional baseball game. Two men sitting several rows in front of us began to argue and shout at each other. I immediately began to tremble and sweat profusely. My chest tightened and I felt weak.

At the time, I was unaware of the reason for my reaction. In retrospect, I realize the incident was triggering in me fears created by a terrible fight between my stepbrother and my father when I was a child. Their fight involved more than shouting. They hit one another and police came to our house. That day my brother was sent away to live with my grandmother.

---

[80] The amygdala.

Although the men at the game were not people I knew and even though they never came to blows, the shouting alone was enough to trigger in me the whole emotional reaction from my childhood.

I needed to "process" these feelings through my understanding in a way that caused me to realize my reaction was not in tune to the present-day situation but one that belonged to something in my past. To accomplish this, I had to grieve the loss of seeing two people I loved deeply try to hurt each other. I had to grieve the overall lack of harmony in my family as well as the loss of my brother's presence in my life. We had been close.

A present-day trigger to the brain calls forth a packaged response based on another time and place in the person's life. The trigger can be set off even if the present event has only a mild resemblance to the original occurrence. Only a few similarities are necessary to trigger the brain's automatic responses to a past event.

Here is another example. One day my husband, Gary, was teaching our son to ride his bike. I watched them from the window. I began to feel afraid and out of control. One part of my brain wanted to stop Gary from teaching Andrew to ride the bike. I felt panic. I imagined something dreadful would happen to Andrew on that bike. At the same time, another part of my brain was saying, "It's OK. He is going to be fine!"

Here were my choices in that moment. I could have forbidden my son from riding the bike. I could have gotten angry with my husband and accused him of pushing our son to do something unsafe. I could have stuffed the whole thing and developed a headache. Or, I could have questioned why I was responding in this way and begin to investigate my own reaction. When a response seems out of proportion to a life event, this last choice is a very good one to investigate.

Fortunately for my son and husband, I questioned the intensity of my response. I took the time to think about my feelings. I suddenly remembered the first day I learned to ride a bike. I practiced until I felt confident enough to try rolling down a hill. I pushed the bike to the top of a hill and with great excitement began a rapid descent.

Whether it was the newness of the experience or the thrill of speed, I don't know, but as I approached the bottom of the hill, I suddenly discovered I couldn't remember how to make the bike stop! I had put so much attention towards getting it to go, I had never thought much about making it stop.

At the bottom of the hill I wiped out right in front of a car which sat at the stop sign. Fortunately, I had no greater injury than scraped knees and wounded pride.

I felt out of control the day my bike sped down that hill. To say that incident with the bike was the only time I felt my life whirling out of control would minimize one of my important early life "themes". Habitual "out of control" situations in my life like sexual, physical and emotional abuse created an atmosphere where a wild bike ride didn't heal with my skinned knees. Instead it became a symbol in my brain of a life pattern.

It is easy to see how people develop severe control problems and seek to take charge of everyone's feelings and choices around them. The cure for such control problems is not to find people who will let you dominate; rather it is to identify the profound feelings of powerlessness and lack of control which created the unresolved grief in the first place. Our losses have two sides, one involves the evil done to us; the other involves the ways we have cooperated with that evil and gone on to perpetrate it towards ourselves and others.

A close friend of mine grew up in a very nice family. There were no shouting matches or hidden abuse. The politeness of family members impressed me. But my friend, Bruce, didn't appear to be living up to his potential. He had great ideas and a wonderful work ethic but everywhere you looked in his life you noticed one thing: here was a guy who was habitually overlooked. He was treated as a workhorse who would get the job done. He ended up performing tasks far above his pay scale but was never recognized or rewarded appropriately for it.

When he came to me for help, we decided that he was doing the work of someone getting paid twice his salary. As we talked about his, we saw a pattern emerge of him being overlooked. Although his home life was very safe, stable, and orderly, there was little relational or emotional connection. There was no recognition of his talents and abilities, or how he was different from his siblings. In brief, he was neglected.

So long as he cooperated with what was expected, no one spent much time or effort finding out what he thought or how he felt. His active mind developed all types of fantasies where he was noticed and appreciated. But the reality of his life never became any of the fantasies. Instead, each job he found seemed to lock him into the role of a minor character, always hoping to have more impact, but seemingly hidden from the notice of his colleagues.

Not surprisingly, he repeated this pattern in the churches he attended. He was quickly identified in that setting as a reliable person who could be counted on to do things, and not make any demands. He always had a place, albeit unnoticed, in the groups in which he was involved, but his heart longed for the responsibility of being a leader. After some ministry time, together, we uncovered this pattern. Bruce has since begun to stand up and be heard at work and church in a way he had never done before. He got a promotion in his company and before long ended up in leadership at the church.

The unresolved grief in Bruce was centered on his view of himself, inherited from the significant people in his childhood. He saw himself as a quiet, proper, and well-mannered person who didn't make many demands and worked hard to keep others happy. He lost out on the opportunity to develop his own ideas and direction when he settled for being mommy and daddy's little obedient child.

I am not down on obedient children, but abject compliance from a child is not as healthy as it looks. Some of the most confused and wounded people I have helped over the years are the "compliant children" who spent their lives trying to keep mom and dad happy or the family together. They have suffered a terrible loss of never being themselves, but just a projection of what someone else wanted them to be.

Another way this "compliance" injures a person is from the perception in the child that they are taking care of the parent by keeping him/her happy rather than feeling the flow of care coming from parent to child. This is a sick type of role reversal, even if it is only in the way the child sees his/her life. In other words, the parents may not be demanding or expecting at all that the child take care of them, but inside the child a set of perceptions and reactions fabricates a no-win situation where in order to receive, the child must always and forever give.

The wounded child in each of us will continue to insist on payment from others, blaming them for our anger and pain until we recognize our losses and their roots. With good grief, we can resolve those losses and have God take over where others have failed us.

In all these examples, Bruce's, mine, and Rebecca's, the cure for the unresolved grief issues is a renewing of the mind. First the emotional process of grief happens and then the more cognitive change in belief systems comes next. Brain studies confirm this. They say that a person must rewire the past experiences by recognizing the present experiences as triggers to the past. They must then process the understanding of how "that was then, and this is now" through the more developed cognitive centers of the brain. The feelings invoked by the present situation are applied to the past and seen as fruits of those former times rather than as appropriate reactions to the present. This I believe is one of the ways that we are called to renew our minds with truth.

Notice I said that first the emotional process of grief happens. This is because the effectiveness of solely cognitive forms of therapy are being called into question because they don't have this back and forth between the emotional brain and thinking brain that is needed. The left brain, where we hold our belief systems, will not revise those beliefs unless engaged by a

99

relational or emotional event. Those events happen in the right brain and the grieving process uses that part of the brain.

Chapter 16—Short List of Unresolved Grief Issues

Every person I have used to illustrate grief has been a composite of many people whom I have helped over the years. Working with my clients and their struggles as well as addressing my own problems, gave me a list of what I see as the major unresolved grief issues. The problems arising from these issues plague people's lives until properly addressed. When they face their need, grieve their loss, and let go of the self-protection measures they employed to guard themselves from loss, resolution comes. Here is my short list of unresolved grief issues.

1.   I am not wanted.
2.   I have been displaced in my parent's affections by another.
3.   I have been abandoned and must take care of myself.
4.   I am rejected for who I am.
5.   I have been negated as a source of information, particularly about myself and my feelings.

I am not wanted.

Jill imagined before she even met people that they would reject her. So, she avoided others and when she had to interact, she kept up her defenses. Occasionally when the loneliness became unbearable, she would try to say what she thought others wanted to hear. It still left her true self disguised, isolated, and lonely.

Her parents had not wanted any more children, but she arrived when they were in their 40's. Her siblings were all much older and she spent much time alone, entertaining herself. When she did interact with her parents and siblings, she was treated as a bother and not welcomed.

Jill had to face the loss of not being wanted. She needed to face how she had tried to protect herself by rejecting others before they could reject her. She also had to look at her way of being phony to try to please others and win their favor. She had put a defensive layer around herself to guarantee no rejection could enter. This, unfortunately, protected her too well. It also kept out any positive attempts others might have tried to make to get to know her. She contributed to the fulfillment of her belief that she was not wanted.

I have been displaced in my parent's affections by another

Jack was the leader of a small Christian ministry. Jack couldn't stand anyone competing with his ministry. He always felt deeply insulted by people not recognizing or contributing to his ministry. He believed it was one of a kind, better than others and worthy of the attention of other Christians far and wide. He truly believed there must be something wrong with them that they didn't acknowledge the wisdom and power of God working through his ministry. He would have his prayer group pray and ask God to convince pastors and church leaders to recognize and desire to include his ministry in their programs and support it.

He constantly mentored people to work with him, but when his helpers became successful, Jack found a reason to dismiss them. He would constantly choose some person to be his favorite, telling them he would hone them to replace him and take over the ministry when he was gone. But when they began to show promise and develop their giftings, he always found fault with them. He even confessed to one of them "When you are up front, I don't feel special anymore." It never occurred to him that he was envious of the talent and success of others.

Jack had to compete with many siblings growing up. He had to constantly prove his point and convince others that he was right and should be heard. He wanted to feel special. He worked hard everywhere he went to gain attention and be recognized. This ministry was something that could distinguish him from the others. Jack never recognized his striving and diligent work ethic as a desperate endeavor to gain the favor of his parents. He had covered his unresolved grief issues with a lifetime of hard work, sacrifice and worst of all, the image that all he was doing was really for God and others. He truly believed he was justified in bullying others to promote his ministry. After all, it was "God's ministry" and almost any means justified the ends of making His ministry successful.

102

I have been abandoned and must take care of myself

Judy always had to make sure that no one was picking up the slack for her. She would refuse to ask for help because it was a great embarrassment to need others. The thought of exposing herself as weak or dependent made her feel ill. She was constantly caring for friends and family but never letting anyone know when she needed help. Every holiday and family get-together were at her house and she bore the brunt of most of the work. At the same time, Judy was backing anyone off from helping her, she wondered why no one seemed to care about her needs. She resented having all the work "dumped" on her and secretly held strong hostility for everyone she "sacrificially" helped. Unfortunately, she never saw herself as the problem. She truly believed that others were just being selfish and that eventually they would be won over by her good modeling of selfless service. She had been waiting for others to change for twenty years and, so far, no one had.

Judy was the middle child in a needy family. She decided at a young age to try and fill in all the gaps that were lacking in her parents. She cared for younger siblings and tried to be a friend to both her parents. She was an honor student and often cooked and cleaned for her mother. She helped her father find a rehab for her older brother. Judy had been in an incubator as an infant. She fought back from near death as a premature baby. She had a big heart and great courage, but from those earliest days the enemy of her soul had caught her in a horrible lie: I must take care of myself and strive to make my world safe. She couldn't see that even as a child her hard work to make the family better was really the concentrated effort to create a protected, orderly living space for herself.

I am rejected for who I am

Dean had only one memory from his childhood. He was standing in his crib waiting for someone or something to happen, he wasn't sure what. The next thing he remembered was in junior high and liking a girl. He tried on several occasions to speak to her, but she looked at him as if he were weird. In conversations, Dean always talked about superficial things: sports, cars

103

weather and girl's bodies. He had totally lost contact with his real heart and desires and longings. By twenty he had decided that sex was the answer to whatever he needed. He had no ability to form any kind of lasting relationships or friendships. His idea of success was to find someone to sleep with. Even while he pursued this lifestyle, he felt great shame about it. He had given his heart to Christ as a teen at a special concert he attended with a friend. A small voice kept trying to get his attention. Finally, one day he listened to it and began to try and remember something from his childhood. He wanted to find that part of himself that could hope and care about others.

He called his mother, something he hadn't done in months and asked her some questions about his early life. His father had died when he was a year old. His mother immediately went to work and left him in a day care. His mother began to cry as she confessed that Dean so reminded her of his father that she couldn't bear to be with him. He spent endless hours at the day care and even when that was over, she often left him at her sister's. Dean's mother gave him a key that day, a key to help him understand the pattern of his life. Besides feeling abandoned by his parents, he had also internalized the terrible lie that something about him was "detestable." His childlike understanding couldn't sort out the family tragedy or that his mother rejected him because of his resemblance to his father. All he knew was that he was rejected, unwanted by the person whom he needed most.

> I have been negated as a source of information,
> particularly about myself and my feelings

Dawn had to give up her job. She was heavily medicated with several drugs to keep her from killing herself. For years, she had suffered depression and anxiety. She wondered if she would have to move back home with her parents. That would not be easy. Her mother was a difficult person to keep happy. Even when away from her mother Dawn could constantly hear "tapes" in her head of mother's advice and rebukes. The confusing thing was that sometimes mother's tapes would contradict each other.

"Life is short, so eat and drink and enjoy life. But "Watch out what you eat, or you'll get fat."

"Why are you always busy and running around doing errands instead of spending time with me?" But "Why are you always idle—sitting and staring at me? Can't you find something to keep yourself occupied?"

Dawn felt that her mother owned her life. She made her take vitamins and drink horrible juices. Her mother seemed to know better than her when she was tired, afraid, depressed or in need. Dawn strangely felt inhabited by her mother.

As a child, Dawn tried to comply with her mother. She felt closer to her mother than anyone else. If Mom said to "have fun" then she would dance and sing and try to look happy. If Mom was in a bad mood, Dawn would try to cheer her up. Her highly sensitive nature was constantly in tune to Mom's feelings. At around thirteen years old, Dawn tried to make other friends, but her mother always convinced her that there was something wrong with them. Dawn was afraid of people and these warnings confirmed her fears. So, she stayed alone. Finally, when she could stand the aloneness no longer, she joined a writing club at school. One day a week she would meet with a small group of students and read each other's poems and essays. This enraged her mother, but Dawn loved the club so much she couldn't bring herself to quit.

Suddenly, her mother became exceedingly hostile to Dawn. Whereas for years the mother has praised Dawn for being the perfect child, now nothing she did seemed to be right. The way she dressed, the ways she walked and styled her hair were all silly. Dawn went from being brilliant to stupid, in her mother's eyes.

Unable to see anything wrong with her mother, Dawn began to wonder what terrible thing had happened to her to so quickly turn her into such a monster. She began to spiral into a deep depression. This brought more negative commentary from her mother. Before long, not only did Dawn quit her writing club but school as well. A tutor came to her home and helped her to complete her junior year. Her aloneness again set in.

Soon Dawn lost interest in most things. Around this time her mother stopped the constant criticism. But now she began telling her family and friends that Dawn was probably crazy and needed medicine. She took Dawn to a specialist who prescribed several different medicines. At the same time, Dawn's mother gave her daughter her meds, she would berate her and claim that she herself never had to deal with her problems through drugs. Dawn would just nod her head and swallow the pills.

Dawn left home against the wishes of her mother. She felt better when she was alone. She got a job as a data entry clerk. Sometimes while falling asleep at night she would remember her poetry and writing and long to share it with someone. But who could she trust? People were scary. Finally, the job was even too much for Dawn's fragile mental condition. Now she was faced with the dilemma of having to return home.

Hope for Dawn could only begin by a separation from her mother's feelings and viewpoint. She had used her mother as an absolute in her life. The ruler she used to measure herself and her life was terribly twisted and bent. No wonder Dawn was caught in mixed messages and despair. Her mother had been her "god" who in the end wasn't meeting her needs. Serving her mother had left her depressed, anxious, suicidal, and without meaning.

Dawn needed a new absolute, the real God. Sadly, many people with Dawn's background find churches that also negate them as a source of information about themselves. Almost cult-like, some sick church systems encourage people to try to forget their humanness and live in a superficial realm of religious platitudes and pat answers.

Here are some other common unresolved grief issues:

1.   I have been ignored, particularly my true self.
2.   My needs for approval, attention, affection, self-worth, belonging, connection, etc. have been neglected.
3.   I have been abused physically, emotionally or sexually.

4.   I have been used as a surrogate parent instead of being allowed to be a child.

5.   I have never been noticed, the real me seems to be invisible.

6.   I am noticed but I am despised.

7.   I fluctuate between being noticed but despised, and then being invisible.

It is truly amazing to me how people recreate these losses in their adult lives until they are resolved. Recently someone came to me with the following "problem": she only liked her husband when he was off traveling. We asked for the presence of the Lord Jesus to come to us and show us where this pattern began in her life. She remembered her father had left to go to war when she was young. She had dreamed about what it would be like if only he were home. This comforted her while he was gone, but when he returned, his brusque and callous attitude towards her destroyed her fantasy.

We asked the Lord Jesus who is the same yesterday, today, and forever to take her back to the feelings she had at this young age in her life. At this point, my friend began to cry and say she felt very afraid. I allowed her to cry for a little while and then I had her say: "Lord Jesus, I am very afraid. I need a father, but my father doesn't seem to know how to love me. I need you to love me."

We then discussed how she had shut out her husband with a hefty dose of anger left over from her relationship with her father. She repented of using this to protect herself from the pain and loss of having felt abandoned by her father emotionally. We asked Jesus to come to her in this place and prayed for all footholds of the enemy in this area of her soul to leave. We discussed what "habits" she would have to break, with the help of the Holy Spirit, to change her attitude and actions towards her husband.

Because she was willing to face this loss and grieve it, she resolved it by letting go of her answer to her need and receiving the love of Christ and His fullness in that place. An infilling of Christ and communion with him is essential for change. Sometimes people will spend years hardening themselves to their losses. Even though they have avoided the pain of the

107

loss they have not avoided effects of the loss. It still insidiously infuses a silent theme into their lives that they can't escape.

Others of a more emotional sort will spend much time crying and raging over their losses, but not really resolving them because they are not willing to face how they have protected themselves and cooperated with a lie. Some just don't have enough faith to trust God to give them what they lack. Ultimately, another relationship is needed to replace what was needed but never provided during our past. We will either surrender ourselves into the arms of God to give us that relationship, or we will continue to replicate broken relationships to try to resolve our issues ourselves.

I am sure that no book or booklet can contain all the different ways that human beings have suffered losses or reacted to their losses. When we accept that we were created to live in a perfect world in unbroken communion with God, our sufferings come into a different light. I hear people trying to shame those who openly try to grieve their losses, saying such things as: "Oh, you don't know what suffering is! Think of those people in countries where they are in prison for their faith. And what about all the starving, homeless people in the third world?"

Let's look at that line of reasoning briefly. So, because I have judged other's pain greater than my own, I have no right to admit that I am hurting or that my pain has validity? Only the "worst" case scenarios are true losses. This requires a hardening of heart towards what are considered "minor" losses. That results in a refusal to feel pain because the mind can't justify a serious enough reason for it. This also ends up being a defense mechanism to avoid pain.

Recognizing the sick patterns of our lives is the first step towards being healed of them. Taking responsibility for our choices based on our losses and grieving them is the next important milestone in this process. By facing our losses directly, grieving them and then seeking the face of God and inviting his Presence where we have had loss is the true point of healing for all our lacks.

So how does God fit into being part of the solution we need? This is the topic of the next chapter.

Chapter 17—God's Presence is the Cure

I work with people who have been traumatized in various ways through abuse and neglect or simply by living with imperfect people who can never provide love as God meant for us to be loved. Coming to know and appropriate God's presence in their lives wherever they have suffered losses brings healing and a greater communion with God. The person they were always meant to be in Christ begins to emerge. They develop and become capable of loving themselves and others with what they have encountered with God.

> Do not conform any longer to the pattern of this world,
> but be transformed by the renewing of your mind.
> Then you will be able to test and approve what God's will is—
> his good, pleasing and perfect will.[81]

This procedure for "curing" inappropriate emotional reactions emerged many years ago, in the Word of God through the apostle Paul. You see, we all carry around in our hearts many patterns of this world based on life experiences which we endured without knowing God was with us. Even as a Christian, there may be many moments and situations of our lives where we are totally lacking in faith to believe God is present.

In the last chapter, I told you about the day I crashed my bike. Back then, I was not aware that God was with me. I couldn't see His love for me. All I felt was paralyzing fear. It was only as I revisited that moment via my feelings (triggered by my son learning to ride a bike) that I could experience and apply the truth of God's presence with me.

I would like to mention here that people who have an ability to feel God's presence already have an advantage in moving rapidly through the grieving process. Others who can't easily feel Him near need more specialized help to do so.

---

[81] Romans 12:2

As for myself, as I dealt with the "bike memory", I also had to recognize it was just the tip of an iceberg representing control problems and my complicity in them. I had been trying to control many things through my life. I had operated out of a type of "hyper-vigilance" in my endeavor to anticipate and manage the constant "dangers" of life.

I had to repent of living like an orphan who had only herself to depend upon. Only by identifying this loss, grieving it with God's presence making me safe enough to do so, and turning away from my reactions based on my loss could I have a restoration of my soul.

I needed God, not just my own protection devices. I was using my own fearfulness to try to protect myself! This was sorrowfully ineffective. Fear flees and God's perfect love[82] comes in when we choose to let go of trying to keep it all together in our own strength. God is available to those who call on Him.

How many of our present-day reactions and perceptions are embedded in the past? How many moments of godlessness (being without an awareness of God) have we experienced in our lives which need a renewing of the mind? Many more, I think, than we would care to admit. The truth is, we are generally lacking in wisdom concerning these things. We stumble through life deaf, dumb, and blind concerning why we do what we do, or feel what we feel. There is a certain deadness that pulls us down.

> He who gets wisdom loves his own soul;
> he who cherishes understanding prospers.[83]

Most of the time, we don't consider that how we view a situation, or a person may not be accurate. We don't think about the possibility that we may be interpreting people and events based upon unresolved losses in our past.

---

[82] See 1 John 4:18
[83] Proverbs 19:8

Two forces fight inside of us. On the one hand, we want to suppress and avoid the pain that we have hidden. But there is also a yearning to reconcile these past losses, to right our past wrongs. This desire is so deeply embedded within us that we often can't isolate it or define it and can't recognize that it is there. These opposing goals battle inside us and weaken us since a house divided against itself cannot stand. Allowing ourselves to admit our perceptions may be seeing through a lens of our past will open the door for the natural desire for healing and truth to emerge.

The above examples are not the only types of situations where unresolved losses can be exerting powerful influence upon us. Our sin is closely linked to it. Let me explain.

The world is constantly seeking to explain away sin as an illness. As the modern theory goes, we have been victimized and are not responsible for what we do. At the other extreme are some Christians who reject all psychological techniques and insights, believing that they are of the devil. Everything comes from our sin, they say, and we just need to repent and these sins, by God's help, will all disappear. The concept of unresolved grief shows us a different way of viewing ourselves in relation to our problems, our sin, and their cure, from a deeply Biblical perspective.

Our lives are affected by two types of losses. One type of loss is created by our decisions to do our own thing and leave God out of the picture. The second type of loss involves others' decisions to leave God out of the picture and sin which cause pain and loss to us.

Remember Rebecca from our earlier chapter? On the one hand, Rebecca had been rejected and abandoned by her family and had suffered loss at their hands. On the other hand, she spent an enormous amount of energy licking her wounds, expressing anger, and rejecting people around her. This created losses for them as well as for her. The two types of losses in her life were deeply related in that they both were caused by poor decisions contrary to God's way of doing things (He is love). Both losses needed to be recognized and died to by the grieving process.

The basis of all sin is independence of God. Why can we say this? Because we are all God's creation, created by Him for the express purpose of depending upon Him, having fellowship with Him, and living to accomplish His will for us. What keeps us from fulfilling His purposes is a desire to be independent of God. As we become Christians, by responding to His mercy, we repent of this independence and begin a long process of surrendering all the areas of our lives to God and His will.

What this means practically, is that whereas we used to strive to meet our own needs in our own power, we now look to Him to meet our needs. Therefore, it is a blessed thing, a good thing to be needy and powerless--or to put it in Jesus's own words-- "poor in spirit." If we do so, we are promised to gain the Kingdom of God within us, which is "fullness in Christ". Jesus Christ Himself becomes the way for us to live, the life by which we live it, and the truth that sets us free from our life without God.[84]

Many people cringe when you talk about "facing reality." In truth, if we reach the point of clarity caused by resolving our losses, reality becomes our best friend and a cause for great joy. We finally see ourselves as we truly are a beloved, cherished, honored creation of a powerful, loving Creator.

> But seek first his kingdom and his righteousness,
> and all these things will be given to you as well.[85]

It is not a sin to want to be provided for. It is normal and natural to desire food, shelter, safety and a sense of belonging to a group who cares about us. These are appropriate needs that are part of being human.

Jesus Christ came and tasted of this humanity and of this neediness. We know he had physical desires because he was hungry and tired and troubled by what he knew he would experience when everyone, especially His

---

[84] See John 14:6.
[85] Matthew 6:33.

Heavenly Father, deserted him. The difference between Jesus and us, however, is that He never attempted to meet these needs outside of God's provision for Him, even though He was tempted to do so. His was a life where He perfectly practiced the presence of God.

He waited on God and depended on God for everything. If something was denied (such as when the Spirit led Him into the desert to fast 40 days), He believed that even His deprivation in the desert was ordained by God for His purposes. His was a life which had no godlessness. Every one of His human needs was met by the Father. Even in His death He gave himself over to this powerlessness and committed Himself into the hands of the Father. His human flesh was full of the Holy Spirit. There was never any agenda but God's agenda in His thinking, His emotions, and His will.

Rebecca needed a different way of relating to people. Theories and standards at a mental level would not change the destructive relational patterns that had plagued her life. She needed to unlearn her ways and learn new ways. A biblical explanation of this is called "dying to the self." It is a transformational process of letting go of our ways and an embracing of God's way. It is a putting to death the hope that our own protection and control are saving our lives and a relinquishing to God's protection and control. I hate it when people assume "dying to self" is a rejection and dismissal of our basic personhood. Let's not forget the beloved person that God wants to be with forever and for whom He sacrificed all.

Our way puts us or other people at the center of the universe to make things right. The results of this way in Rebecca's life was anger and disappointment towards others, and loneliness and isolation for herself. Her self-protection had not in the end protected her. Her demands that others change their responses to her to make her life right were ruining her relationships. How could Rebecca unlearn these ways? How could she die to these perceptions when that was all she knew?

Our troubles can be a great door of hope for us if we will let them. Allowing ourselves to face loss and grief is the passageway to healing and health.

114

Crossing the desert of grief leads to a new promise land of strength and vitality.

The grieving process, built into us by God, can turn trouble in our lives around to work for our good. The grieving process allows us to be weaned from our own ways and free to embrace God's ways. The grief process allows a gradual letting go of "the way it was supposed to be" and opens a door to a new way. In Part 1 we outlined how to grieve and emphasized the safety needed for it. We need assurance we will be loved even when we admit and express negative emotions.

Viewing ourselves or others as the answer to life's problems is a form of idolatry. We turn from idolatry and disengage ourselves from it by moving through the stages of grief. We begin by recognizing that our ways of meeting our own needs are dead and this causes us to let go of them. We admit our powerlessness to establish salvation in our own lives. We admit our wrong at having demanded that others make our lives right.

In this place of emptying ourselves of our plans and ambitions, we come to a point of surrendering to God's way and the possibility of emerging into the Divine blueprint already in place within us. Here we let Him comfort us in our grief, change our thinking and show us the lies we have believed as well as the truth we need to set us free. A whole new level of energy is available to us at the end of the grieving process. It is energy that used to keep the negative emotions on hold.

He is our Shepherd and because of that we will not stay in need. Here is a prayer you can start with in your journey to know God. Sit and quiet yourself each day and ask the Holy Spirit to help you receive God's love and perspective.

"Heavenly Father, I don't have all that I need. I have tried many ways to get what I need on my own but have failed to satisfy my soul. Jesus experienced humanity so He could understand and help me. Please come to me now and give me His life and help through the Holy Spirit. Help me to let go of my own perceptions and demands. Help me to have faith to trust you to take care of me. Thank you for your promise that you will never leave me or forsake me. No matter what losses I have had in life, always let me finish in Your Divine Embrace as I let them go. In Jesus name, Amen."

As we launch into a new way of living, we will find ourselves revisiting an established path within us: the way of becoming like a little child, which is the next topic we want to address.

Chapter 18—Like a Little Child

Many people who have come to me live their lives as if they are an orphan. Sometimes the perception of not being wanted was based on a temporary disappointment. Sometimes it was a total lie they believed without explanation. Wherever the message came from if the result is that you are living like you have no one who really cares for you, then you see yourself as an orphan and that will hamstring your efforts to connect with God and others.

You will help to create an environment around you that further encourages the perception that you are truly an orphan. Even when others approach you with kindness or concern, you may be unable to trust them. This will create constant loneliness and disappointment and a terrible sense of not being wanted. Only in uncovering the lie and grieving the losses will you be set free from your self-inflicted orphanage.

Here is another illustration of that "orphan" lifestyle.

Bob was convinced that life was not worth living and had tried to commit suicide several times. We began to ask the Lord Jesus to begin revealing how Bob perceived his life and where that perception originated. We discovered this came from his womb experience. Bob was the first child after his mother had a series of miscarriages. Somehow, he had perceived that his mother's womb was a place of death and felt guilty that he had lived while his siblings had died. He was reacting to a lie that said everything was his fault. His mother's problems were somehow because of him. He imagined other people to be victimized by his very existence. His response was to try to redeem the mistake of his life by taking it. The only way to live, Bob thought, was to die.

I believe many people who are caught in destructive addictions have a similar belief system to Bob's. Life seems like a game that they can never win. For Bob, deliverance came as a series of acceptances that he had played God over his own life and needed to accept God's will that he should live

I helped him to grieve the loss of those siblings who died before him. I assured him they were in heaven waiting to meet him when God decided he should go. Bob also had to grieve the fact that he didn't have control over or responsibility for everyone else's feelings. He came to see that viewing everything as his fault was a way of avoiding powerlessness and a way of staying in control. If everything was his fault, then he was in the driver's seat. He didn't have to count on anyone else to give him significance. He viewed himself as having great significance, albeit negative significance. But negative significance was viewed as better than no significance at all. He was at the center of his world.

We who are Christians have a new life given to us in the second birth (being born again) and we are meant to grow in it, re-experiencing the child-like faith that the world and our lives extinguished in us.

The Holy Spirit wants to cultivate His life in us. It won't happen just in mere theory. We need to know at the practical level how to lay hold of all God has for us. The process of grief is the way to a new life.

> May God himself, the God of peace,
> sanctify you through and through.
> May your whole spirit, soul and body be kept blameless
> at the coming of our Lord Jesus Christ.
> The one who calls you is faithful, and he will do it.[86]

The understanding of unresolved grief is true wisdom. Jesus said being a little child before God is a prerequisite to entering His kingdom.[87] Another way to say it is that for the kingdom of God to enter a part of our soul, we need to become like a small child. This is because children are dependent by nature. Here is a list of what that looks like:

1. They are needy, powerless, humble, teachable and willing to trust and make themselves open to relationship.

---

[86] 1 Thessalonians 4:10.
[87] Matthew 18:1.

118

2. They also quickly grieve loss and go on, if allowed.
3. They automatically assume that they are unable to meet their own needs and must look to someone else.

This is what is required of us to live in God's kingdom and to have His kingdom flourish and grow in us. Every area of our lives must come to Him in dependency as a little child. This is total foolishness in the world's eyes, by the way.

> There is a way that seems right to a man,
> but in the end, it leads to death.[88]

Remember Rebecca's story from the beginning of Part 2? Rebecca felt justified in harboring anger and resentment towards others for their reactions to her. She believed she had every right to blame the people around her for her problems. This was a way that seemed right to her, but it ended in death: death to her relationships, death to her hope for change, death to peace. Rebecca needed to face where she had not depended on God and how she had replaced him by faith in herself and others. This could be traced back to her childhood when she was so very powerless and dependent.

If you have children, you can be a facilitator of much healing for them by taking their feelings seriously. Loving eye contact, a listening ear and gentle (non-sexual) touch can do wonders to restore your child's soul. Sometimes they just misbehave, but other times their "overreactions" are ways of saying: "I have a loss here that I don't understand and can't resolve." Insight and compassion from us can settle problems now that could otherwise plague them for many years as adults.

We can be the ambassador of God's love and care for people in our lives God wants to replace all the hurt, fear, and empty places of their lives with

---

[88] Proverbs 14:12

.

His presence, assurance and fullness. Then they can grow into the fullness of the beautiful person He has created them to be.

It is the losses experienced in our early life and the belief system that emerges from them that affect our adult life. It is our first impressions of self and others that guides our present perceptions and reactions. It is the early experiences that teach us a philosophy of life that may be exceedingly contrary to God's word. But this is where we must begin.

So many Christians take a quantum leap of denial from "the old life" to "the new life in Christ." They expect to pour true spirituality out of a box and into an empty bowl, like freeze dried potato flakes, mix water and stir poof! A mature, sanctified Christian is created! They fail to realize that Paul wrote his Epistles to believers in whom "Christ was not yet formed".

The amazing provision of heaven wants to fall on us but is there room inside of us to receive it? If the Father's love bounces off us because we are so fill of other "stuff", then what are we to do?

My co-worker, Richard Kinney, received an impartation of the Father's love that has done a miraculous work in restoring his childlike hope from the harm done by having been abandoned by both parents when he was six months old. He often prays for others to receive this same impartation.

Earlier I taught about the role of resignation in the life of someone Richard was counseling. Richard saw how the Father's love couldn't seem to penetrate the soul of the counselee. He saw that layers of resignation had formed a hard crust in the person's soul. It was covering up hopeless/despair which the person did not believe they could face. The soul full of such things as resignation and hopeless/despair will have little ability or room to receive the Father's love. These negative responses to dashed hopes through our lives will jam up our capacity for soaking up the love that God has for us as well as the love available from our present-day significant others.

Here is Richard's explanation of resignation:

Mostly this happens in childhood, when you are plunged into a situation that is so intense for you that you experience the intense emotion of hopeless/despair. To me it's like a black cyclone with a howling wind blowing through it, and very sharp pain.

What happens is, the enemy will come and offer protection from that almost unbearable pain if you'll agree for him to install a floor of resignation over it. So, most of us say 'yes', and honestly if that was the only choice between hopeless/despair or resignation, resignation would be the choice to take, for sure.

But that's not the only choice now. As adults we can rid ourselves of the hopeless/despair, which runs around inside of us like rats in the basement causing trouble, taking our energy. Having that toxic evil inside of us still costs us something even if we're not experiencing it now. We can ask Jesus, "Come and pull that hopeless/despair out of me and rid me of it." When it comes up, that's a good thing. It would be like if the rat showed itself and you shot it.

Secondarily, the resignation needs to be broken up and everything else beneath it cleaned out. It's like a crust, and underneath almost everyone I'm working with is finding layer upon layer of almost like a sod, the dirt and the grass, that they're stacking up one on top of the other. That creates a spiritual substance that weighs us down. It keeps us stuck on the earth.

I've been talking to people about entering the rest of God and most people can't do that because they're so heavy, they're stuck on the earth. Think of the giant rockets that are needed to launch a space capsule up out of the gravity of earth. But once it climbs beyond the pull of gravity, tiny little bursts of jets will push them all over the place very easily.

A person who's entered the rest and ceased from their own works to some degree means ceasing from the heaviness of the trauma and the things that you carry. This allows you to accomplish much with tiny bursts of energy as lead by the Holy Spirit. You will have fun, have rest and peace, and your body will show the effects of living in a no-gravity situation.

In summary, we want to enter the rest of God in every area of our souls. We want to be free from whatever toxins are inhibiting health in our minds, emotions, wills and bodies. We have the Holy Spirit to guide us through this and He may lead us to seek a counselor or group or church to help us with the process.

Even if you are not able yet to trust in His love for you, I know beyond a shadow of a doubt that He is for you and wants to intervene on your behalf. I want to use my faith right now to pray for you that your decision to read this book is an act of faith on your part and that you will see God's further help for you on this path very soon!

I claim this verse for you and know God's commitment in bringing it about:

> May God himself, the God of peace, sanctify you through and through.
> May your whole spirit, soul and body
> be kept blameless at the coming of our Lord Jesus Christ.

For further development and help, you may want to read my next book for the advancement of spirituality in believer's lives: Change Management for the Soul, Volume 1. I have included an excerpt below to give you an idea of its contents.

About the Author

Dr. Nancy Moelk has been counseling, teaching and mentoring people for over 25 years. She and her husband, Gary, spent seven years in France and North Africa as missionaries. After returning home, Nancy began a journey of inner healing which led to her becoming a counselor and trainer of lay ministers and Christian professionals who wanted to incorporate Biblical concepts into their practices. She has taught classes on personal growth and ministry to hundreds of people from several states and from many congregations.

Nancy currently serves as Co-Director of Firehouse Ministries, Inc. with Richard Kinney and ministers to people from all over the country. Visit firehouseministries.com for more information and many resources to encourage your spiritual life. Nancy lives near Atlanta with Gary, her husband. Their lives have been blessed with four grown and married children and 10 grandchildren.

Made in the USA
Columbia, SC
23 February 2021

33425375R00079